# LOVE AND LANGUAGE

# LOVE AND LANGUAGE

## A STUDY OF THE CLASSICAL
## FRENCH MORALIST
## WRITERS

LOUISE K. HOROWITZ

OHIO STATE UNIVERSITY PRESS : COLUMBUS

Copyright © 1977 by the Ohio State University Press
All Rights Reserved.
Manufactured in the United States of America

**Library of Congress Cataloguing in Publication Data**

Horowitz, Louise K
  Love and Language.

  Bibliography: p. 161
  Includes index.
  CONTENTS: The Chevalier de Méré.—La Rochefoucauld.—
Madame de Lafayette.—Saint-Evremond. [etc.]
  1. French literature—17th century—History and criticism.  I. Title.
PQ249.H6                    848'.4'08                    76-57232
ISBN 0-8142-0233-0

TO MY MOTHER AND FATHER

# TABLE OF CONTENTS

## ACKNOWLEDGMENTS

IKE SO MANY SCHOLARS BEFORE me, I wish above all to thank Henri Peyre, whose direction of an earlier version of this work was unfailingly generous. My deep appreciation extends also to Jules Brody and Mary Ann Caws for their critical advice, which was as inspirational as it was practical.

I am grateful to my colleagues at the University of Rochester, Kurt Weinberg and Christopher Lasch, two of the sternest "moralists" I know, for their reading of, and interest in, my manuscript. I should like also to express my gratitude to Michel Benamou and Michel Beaujour, who first stimulated what is now an abiding love of French literature, as well as to my friend Joan Rosasco, who over the years has shared with me the very richest perceptions and ideas.

Finally, I wish to thank my husband, Robert F. Horowitz, for his always pertinent criticism, unquestioning support, and life-renewing sense of humor.

# LOVE AND
# LANGUAGE

# INTRODUCTION

$T$HE DAZZLING ALEXANDRINE verse continues to exert a virtual monopoly in the field of classical French literature. Once seduced by it, the reader may only reluctantly return to prose. Certain novelists, notably Mme de Lafayette, receive some attention, although this is generally limited to *La Princesse de Clèves*. (More students surely read Racine's *La Thébaïde*, even though it is not included among the few truly famous plays, than read the lesser-known works of Mme de Lafayette: *Zaïde* or *La Princesse de Montpensier*.) As for the moralists, with the sole exception perhaps of Pascal, they are traditionally viewed as a rather homogeneous group, whose works are frequently grouped together as one body of thought, their lack of individuality signaling their failure to captivate, to entice.

Moreover, certain among these prose writers continue to be, at least on this side of the Atlantic, virtually neglected. Although Pascal, La Rochefoucauld, Mme de Lafayette, and, to a lesser degree, La Bruyère do filter into the American curriculum, many other writers—the chevalier de Méré, Saint-Evremond, Nicole, Jacques Esprit—are consigned to the pejorative categories of minor or secondary. This value judgment conveniently negates their possible worth and thus frees the student of French literature to concentrate on the brilliance of the classical theater. It is not my intention here to question the exceptional merit of that theater. Rather, in undertaking to study the moralist writers, I seek to show the extraordinary complexity of thought that permeates the individual works, a complexity that too often, in the face of demands for reduction, has disappeared, covered over by generalities.

Considerably more is at stake than a delineation, however precise, of the thought of any one writer, a self-evident fact from the selection of several writers. Nor does this study attempt to summarize the totality of these writers' thinking, which is also obvious from the limited length of each chapter. Instead, this study proposes a "sounding" of one particular preoccupation of the age, that which years later Stendhal would call *l'amour-passion*. No analysis of a single text, nor of one writer, can possibly offer the multiple facets of that problem in the same way as can a study of diverse thinkers, and the question of erotic love in classical French literature suffers if posed from an overemphasis upon an isolated text or author. To counteract such a trend, the opposite tendency, equally limiting, is toward generalization, toward "relevancy." This series of essays concertedly attempts to avoid either of those directions.

It is somewhat of a cliché to state that the preoccupation, the obsession even, with the passions dominated the classical experience. However, critics and students have long fixed upon the theater of Racine as the primary focus of their investigations; and whether the study has been couched in the heavily moralizing expression of *la critique universitaire* or in the deliberately evocative, provocative language of Roland Barthes, the functioning of Eros in the plays has been viewed as the undisputed center of that theater. What has been done for Racine, I seek to do here for several prose writers.

From a series of related but independent essays, what will ideally emerge is a deepened awareness of how in-

[4]

tensely the classical moralists experienced the problem of powerful emotion as a potentially destructive force—both for the individual and the society that enveloped him. The moralists' efforts did not mirror at all the ongoing reality of the era's sexual mores. It was, rather, the task of the memoir-writers to describe that reality; the moralists were concerned with presenting the other side of the problem: control of the erotic experience.

In what terms, then, was this desire for control expressed? What methods could ensure that passion, chaotic and unruly, would be tamed? Reading through the classical moralists' works, one perceives a general movement toward language as one method of moderating the excesses of erotic love. This connection is a loose one, and not at all systematic. Nevertheless, from Méré through Guilleragues (the presumed author of the *Lettres portugaises*), language becomes an active force in the suppression of Eros. Whether the writer is Mme de Sévigné, whose corpus of letters to her daughter may be viewed as an attempt to reform or restructure the love relationship into a more aesthetically, and emotionally, satisfying experience; Saint-Evremond, who cultivated an emotional distance through letters of advice, which allowed for a flirtation with questions of love and sexuality while also permitting a safety zone of escape, the boundaries of the page; or Jacques Esprit, who favored the most rigorous and repressive inner "dialogue"; in all these cases, language became the way to mastery over the undisciplined self. For La Rochefoucauld, in a work recently attributed to him, *La Justification de l'amour*, only love seen as a secret could maintain the code of *l'honnêteté*, the moral system so carefully developed and analyzed by the chevalier de Méré. The fascination with *l'honnête homme*, which marks much of the literature of the *grand siècle*, and which was dependent upon the successful manipulation of form and style, in language particularly, is yet another sign of the ongoing effort to dispel the disruptive impulses of *l'amour-passion*.

For two of the writers studied here, the problem goes

still further. Showing the ultimate failure of language to control at all, they propose, consequently, recourse to total silence. Mme de Lafayette and *la religieuse portugaise*, in a direct negation of the hope that the "word" can successfully master erotic energy, offer bitter portrayals of exactly that failure. Language here is viewed as unable to repress successfully the spontaneous impulses of love, for the two domains persistently refuse to mix. But even when the antidote of language is shown as a failure, even when silence is viewed as the sole "out," what cannot be denied is the extraordinary awareness of language at this time. This perception was translated in the theater of the age. Hippolyte's inability to communicate, part of his Amazon heritage, shows to what degree language has been sexualized in Racine's theater. The entire tragedy of *Bérénice* is one of moral "aphasia." This strong consciousness of language should not be neglected, for it forms one of the most essential aspects of the classical literary experience. The moralist writers of the era were caught up in a persistent attempt to define—perhaps to redefine after a cataclysmic period of history—the "self," and it was the power of language that could, it was hoped, not only explicate but create. There is great attention to what can only be called the *factice* in these authors' works. They communicate an urgency to reform the raw material, to transform the private into the societal. The long introductory pages of Mme de Lafayette's *La Princesse de Clèves* form one powerful example of the opposition of these two structures, the glittering brilliance of court society serving to mask the personal, hidden tensions of warring egos.

This study seeks wide diversity in the selection of writers. Nevertheless, it is, by necessity, limited. Although a series of related but independent essays best serves the stated purposes, a distinction should be made between what has been stressed and what has been omitted. Certain moralists are included, and others, often important, are left aside. For what reasons? This study seeks, first of all, to focus upon writers of different intellectual bents. At the same

time, I have attempted to represent various "genres"—
essays, maxims, novels, letters—for the prose works of the
seventeenth century are far from limited to one format.
It is important, moreover, to add here that biographical
information is left aside as not contributing to the subject
and, in fact, possibly detracting from it; for the emphasis
remains throughout not on any one writer but on his or
her analysis of *l'amour-passion*. Furthermore, each chapter
is an interpretation unto itself, related to those that pre-
cede and follow, but deliberately not through any system
of comparisons. And finally, there is a recognition that each
work studied can be viewed from other, different perspectives. What is really proposed here is one person's reading
and evaluation. This, I believe, is the primary task of any
critic—a personal "struggle" with the text.

However, the important question of who was left out and
why needs further elucidation. It is, moreover, a problem
considerably more difficult to justify than the corresponding
one regarding the writers who were included. To a large
extent, the selection of authors was based on the period
of the 1660s and 1670s. The body of writings studied here
do fit largely into that time span (with Saint-Evremond's
and Méré's works traversing a slightly more comprehensive
period). Hence, moralists such as the "mystical" Saint-
François de Sales, or the "libertine" La Mothe le Vayer
are not studied, their works dating from earlier in the
century. La Bruyère, however, has been included, despite
the "generation gap," in a chapter specifically intended as
a conclusion, because his work clearly shows the limits of
the preceding literary generation's enterprise. The *Caractères*, published first in 1688, offer the portrait of a society
less concerned with self-control than with material acquisition. Language in La Bruyère's book no longer tames;
rather, it accumulates, in a moral and spiritual vacuum.

There are factors other than time, however, that limited
the selection of authors. Bossuet, for example, could easily
be included in this "sounding," as could Nicole; and if
they are not, it is only because of certain artificial limits

[7]

that any study places upon itself, as well, perhaps, because of a reluctance to probe writers who demand a thorough knowledge of the subtle depths of Christian theology. In the end there was also the important recognition that certain writers could best exemplify not any specific, preformed thesis (for there is no attempt here to "prove" any formulated-in-advance, tight theory; the study remains consistently a *sondage*) but at least general movements and directions along which any analysis must be oriented.

There are, however, two writers who, although not included in the body of this study, deserve attention, even if of a summary nature: one, Descartes, omnipresent throughout this series of essays, though concealed; and two, Pascal, central to his age, and not included here because of a reluctance to add still more verbiage to the ancient debate over the authenticity of the *Discours sur les passions de l'amour*, and also because of a realization that this work, questions of authorship aside, is not all that original, repeating to a large extent many ideas exposed in several of the chapters in far more striking fashion.

But it is first Descartes who deserves, even demands, some explication, and in particular his work *Les Passions de l'âme*, published at the end of 1649, shortly before his death. Many of the ideas he espouses in this work had already been expressed in his correspondence, notably in that with "la princesse Elisabeth." As early as 1645, Descartes seems to have been preoccupied with defining and explaining his view of man's involvement with strong emotion, and in one letter to Elisabeth clearly posits his belief: "Je ne suis point d'opinion . . . qu'on doive s'exempter d'avoir des passions; il suffit qu'on les rende sujettes à la raison, et lorsqu'on les a ainsi apprivoisées, elles sont quelquefois d'autant plus utiles qu'elles penchent plus vers l'excès."[1] This notion of taming through reason, through self-knowledge and control, is also at the base of *Les Passions de l'âme*, and the work relies heavily upon a constant synthesis between emotional emptiness and untamed passions. Descartes seeks to maintain the perfect measure, the right dosage of emotion, and though *les passions* frequently serve to fortify and maintain concepts and beliefs, they may also risk pushing too far: "Tout le mal qu'elles peuvent causer consiste en ce qu'elles fortifient et conservent ces pensées plus qu'il n'est besoin, ou bien qu'elles en fortifient et conservent d'autres auxquelles il n'est pas bon de s'arrêter."[2]

The "self" that Descartes creates in his work, constantly on guard against emotion that is not understood or directed by the system of will, when touched by love is involved in a process of self-perfection that becomes a goal unto itself, love serving then as only a means. This view of love demands a recognition of superiority in the chosen love object and reflects Descartes' preoccupation with self-discipline and control. What emerges is a picture of a well-disciplined, self-knowledgeable individual, bent on seeking to maintain a controlled form of emotion in his life. Any distance from this basic principle of perfection, such as an ill conceived love, may result in a serious moral downfall: "L'amour qui est injuste nous joint à des choses qui peuvent nuire, ou du moins qui ne méritent pas d'être tant considérées par nous qu'elles sont, ce qui nous avilit et nous abaisse."[3] The theme of potential self-degradation pervades the moralist literature, reminding repeatedly that love can throw into disruption the composed, tight system of self-regulation, that it can disorient, alienate the self. This awareness, which may, as for Madame de Lafayette, translate itself by a vocabulary of "falling," points persistently back to Descartes.

But Descartes himself admits to the possibility of failure in this attempt at "taming" passions: "J'avoue qu'il y a peu de personnes qui se soient assez préparées en cette façon contre toutes sortes de rencontres, et que ces mouvements excités dans le sang par les objets des passions suivent d'abord si promptement des seules impressions qui se font dans le cerveau et de la disposition des organes, encore que l'âme n'y contribue en aucune façon, qu'il n'y a point de sagesse humaine qui soit capable de leur résister

[9]

lorsqu'on n'y est pas assez préparé."[4] Descartes proposes, then, as the definitive remedy in the battle, a constant state of self-preparation, maintained by means of the "reflective" process, by means of an interior dialogue. Thus the word is given the ultimate task of control. If moved to unreason, the sole final recourse must be to the domain of language, to *la réflection* and to *la résolution*, hence to a temporal structure that places its greatest value upon the slow, meditative, recuperative balm of reason, rather than upon the spontaneous immediacy of emotion. The principal component is the "word," always lucid. It is above all this emphasis upon structured language to counteract the disorder and disorientation caused by *les passions* that makes Descartes' work significant in terms of the study proposed here.

The reasons for mentioning the *Discours sur les passions de l'amour*, for so long attributed to Pascal, are not unlike those for *Les Passions de l'âme*. Both works decidedly reflect important trends in the thinking of the age, many of which lend force to what will be studied in the body of this essay. If "Pascal's" short piece was not included there, it was for the reasons mentioned earlier: a wish to avoid adding yet more opinion to the long-standing debate over its authenticity, and secondly (and far more importantly), a developing feeling that the work does not offer the originality and richness one might anticipate. Many of the ideas expressed in the *Discours*, e.g., on the ties between love and ambition, are expressed with far greater force by a writer like the chevalier de Méré. However, because the work is considered a "highlight" of the age, it is necessary to indicate some of the ideas that bear most directly on this study; for whether or not the *Discours* properly belongs to Pascal, it is at least a part of the writings of the age, and hence deserves consideration as a reflection of general trends.

As for the debate over authorship, it is a very old one by now, going back to 1842 and to Victor Cousin's discovery of the manuscript. Cousin, like Lanson and Saulnier after him, was ready to accept the attribution of the work to Pascal. However, Louis Lafuma, returning to a careful and precise study of the sources, adopted another opinion, maintaining that Pascal could not have written the work, for the author apparently made use of texts that did not appear until after Pascal's death in 1662.[5] However, the dispute, obviously unending, although M. Lafuma's conclusions have been accepted by many, is not really of interest here. Rather, it is more important to focus upon those passages of the *Discours sur les passions de l'amour* that reflect dominant directions and currents of the era.

As in Descartes' writings, as in so many of the classical moralists' works, there is in the *Discours* a decided fascination with the perfection sought from the love experience. The association of love with moral superiority, with self-development, runs through the work: "Il semble que l'on ait toute une autre âme quand l'on aime que quand on n'aime pas; on s'élève par cette passion, et on devient tout grandeur."[6] Loving, stripped here of an erotic base, becomes a means to self-recognition, to self-recomposition, through a constant mingling with "reason," an association that the author maintains throughout the work. Love remains, within this context, a tamed force; is tamed, more precisely, within the context of the work.

Moreover, the "rules" of loving are developed in the *Discours* much as in the other *mondain* literature of the age, properly reflecting the semi-literary milieu that produced it. There is a close attention to correct form, to the certitude that the "right" language can communicate love, can thereby assure its success, and the wooing attempts of the male are viewed here as an absolutely integral part of the love situation.

But the most important part of the *Discours sur les passions de l'amour*, and that which forms its central premise, is the close relationship between love and boredom. The work opens with a declaration of direct hierarchy: "L'homme est né pour penser." The passions serve primarily as a stimulus in what would otherwise become a

[11]

monotony of reason. "C'est une vie unie à laquelle il ne peut s'accommoder; il lui faut du remuement et de l'action, c'est-à-dire qu'il est nécessaire qu'il soit quelquefois agité des passions, dont il sent dans son coeur des sources si vives et si profondes."[7] Thus, from the beginning, the role of love has been relegated to second place, necessary only as a lift in an otherwise thinking universe. What stands out is the denial of spontaneity, the extreme sense of regulation, the feeling that "love" is viewed as a rather benign force. "Discoursing" as he does, the author successfully limits, even bans, the spontaneous, disruptive side of erotic energy, and thus tames in advance a potentially chaotic situation.

Although it is true that the authors of *Les Passions de l'âme* and the *Discours sur les passions de l'amour* share with many other writers of their time a core of basic beliefs, what is particularly important in terms of the study proposed here is that these works reflect a fundamental trend of classical moralist writing: the need to analyze love, to structure, to negate, to purge. This need, furthermore, clearly translates a desire to free themselves and their readers from the illusions of love, from the romantic, *romanesque* myth-making (prevalent earlier in the century, but also a long-standing trend of Western thought). One after another, each writer, emphasizing diverse means, seeks liberation from the demands of passion, and it is precisely these diverse ways "out" that this study will attempt to explore.

To insure conformity throughout this work, I have modernized all French spelling, including the quotations from modern editions where editors have chosen to leave certain forms unchanged, as in the *Lettres* of Mme de Sévigné and the *Oeuvres complètes* of the chevalier de Méré.

1. René Descartes, *Les Passions de l'âme* (Paris: Gallimard, 1953; preface, 1969), preface, p. 10.

2. Ibid., p. 80.

3. Ibid., p. 126.

4. Ibid., pp. 175-76.

5. A precise analysis is available in Louis Lafuma's 1950 edition of the *Discours sur les passions de l'amour*, published by Delmas. This scholar conjectures that

the work is by Charles-Paul d'Escoubleau, marquis d'Alluye et de Sourdis. With greater certainty he concludes: "C'était certainement quelqu'un qui fréquentait assidûment plusieurs des vingt ruelles qui animaient la vie littéraire et galante de l'époque" (p. 108).

6. Blaise Pascal, *Discours sur les passions de l'amour* (Paris: Hachette, 1966; original edition, 1897), p. 134.

7. Ibid., p. 123.

Chapter One

# THE CHEVALIER DE MÉRÉ

*T*HE CHEVALIER DE MÉRÉ IS KNOWN anecdotally as the gentleman who one day in 1653 accompanied Pascal (and the duc de Roannez, their mutual friend) on a coach ride, thereby exposing the great mathematician to a whole new way of thinking, which Pascal would call *l'esprit de finesse*, and which represented man's intuitive, perceptive side. Although Méré describes the ride and ensuing conversation in detail (and readily sheds much favorable light on his own role as philosopher-teacher), the incident tends to overshadow careful, thorough study of Méré's works: the *Conversations*, first published in 1668–69; the *Discours*, which appeared in 1676–77; the *Maximes, sentences et réflexions morales et politiques*, published in 1687, and the correspondence.[1]

This is not to deny the mutual influence that Pascal and Méré may have exerted over each other. Or perhaps the ideas they shared are less a result of direct influence than of the force the age's diverse philosophical currents may have exerted on them simultaneously. In any case, Méré's ideas on the two kinds of study needed by man to advance successfully in the world do call to mind Pascal's famous passage on *l'esprit de géométrie* and *l'esprit de finesse*:

Il y a deux sortes d'Etude, l'une qui ne cherche que l'Art
et les Règles; l'autre qui n'y songe point du tout, et qui n'a
pour but que de rencontrer par instinct et par réflexions,
ce qui doit plaire en tous les sujets particuliers. S'il fallait
se déclarer pour l'une des deux, ce serait à mon sens pour
la dernière, et surtout lorsqu'on sait par expérience ou par
sentiment, qu'on se connaît à ce qui sied le mieux. Mais
l'autre n'est pas à négliger, pourvu qu'on se souvienne
toujours que ce qui réussit vaut mieux que les Règles. (2:109)

Like Pascal, moreover, the chevalier was fascinated by
mathematics. Gambling interested him for its rewards, perhaps even more so for its elegant retirement into a closed
circle, removed from less-refined preoccupations (that is,
as the quintessential activity of *l'honnête homme*), but he
was also drawn to the mathematical aspect of the stakes
and worked with Pascal at solving various game problems.[2]
The idea of order that permeates his writings is perhaps a
result of this training; but whatever the reason, Méré,
while relying on intuition in structuring his moral universe,
also believed firmly in an aesthetics of symmetry and proportion: "Tout ce qu'on fait et tout ce qu'on dit est une
espèce d'Architecture: il y faut de la Symmétrie" (2:37).
Thus affective reactions, inherently less organized in their
original state, demand a constant ordering and structuring,
consistent with the chevalier's emphasis on control.

To achieve his ends, the chevalier de Méré relied on
techniques culled both from *finesse* and *géométrie*. But
once this intellectual kinship with Pascal has been established, Méré tends to become a shadow figure, if not for
scholars, at least for the body of students, who become only
marginally acquainted with the moralist tradition. There
may be an additional reason for passing him by. His works
are dry, repetitious, rigid; everything is constrained and
measured. Méré's attention to performance in society runs
counter to current belief in movement and free expression.
The reader is not likely to find much in his work that is
relevant to life as we know it today.

The question then arises whether Méré offered a "rele-

[16]

vant" experience to seventeenth-century Frenchmen. His writings clearly did not propose a code of living in reach of "everyman." Méré, building a moral structure whose goal was social perfection, designed for a superior individual constantly in control of himself, was writing for an elite. His ideas had meaning for that social class which earlier in the century had found in the ethics of glory and grandeur appropriate self-definition. The ideal proposed by the chevalier de Méré is directed toward a generation who had discovered the bankruptcy of the morals of heroism. The nobleman's glory and power were hardly significant concepts at a time of weakening political power. Méré's works, published well into the second half of the century, propose the small-scale, reduced code necessary to such a time, the diminishing of stress on *la vraie vertu* reflecting the decreased political power. Henceforth, social perfection will be the new goal.

Jean Starobinski, in an article on La Rochefoucauld but which applies with equal force to Méré, formulates the transition that has occurred: "C'est dans le champ social lui-même, c'est dans le commerce quotidien que les valeurs esthétiques vont se substituer aux impératifs moraux et prendre à leur tour valeur d'impératifs. L'existence trouvera sa règle dans la loi qui gouverne le rapport harmonieux des formes et des fictions: il faudra apprendre à plaire, à cultiver les agréments, à trouver les airs et les manières."[3]

The acknowledgment that the old rules no longer compose an operable force engenders an alternative moral structure: *l'honnêteté*. Méré's writings are faithfully devoted to the formulation of this idea. His conversations with the maréchal de Clérambault, in their structure alone, especially reflect the preoccupation with refinement and style as they fluctuate between two activities: conversing and gambling, recourse to the latter being the primary interrupting force in the flow of words. It is not only a leisured world that emerges but a facile one, alternating between gentlemanly conversation and *le jeu*.

The emphasis on refined elegance, on manner and cor-

[17]

rect form, demanded an ideal civilization to serve as an example to the seventeenth-century nobility. Méré chose one way beyond the time and space of classical France: ancient Greece. The portrait, not surprisingly, is of a fictitious Greece, heavily romanticized and obviously removed from any historical accuracy. The chevalier offers a superb glorification of a refined, elegant civilization, superior in manners and conduct to any other. He frequently alludes, it is true, to heroes and heroism, but he does not use these terms as Corneille did. Gone are the sublime pride, the heroic stances, the princely declamations, for Heroism is now refinement, and the Hero is he who conquers not violently, but "d'une manière qui plaise" (1:52).

The core of Méré's work, *l'honnêteté*, was not a new subject, having already been analyzed by writers as eminent as Chapelain and Balzac. Méré's direct predecessor was Faret, who, in his *L'Honneste Homme*, published in 1630, sought to establish a code of behavior for aristocratic man at court. But the chevalier's definition went further than his predecessors', and his own involvement with the ideal is more intense. He both enlarged and deepened the concept, separating it from more limited notions of courtly conduct and social gallantry. *L'honnêteté* for Méré was an active force—"il faut qu'elle agisse et qu'elle gouverne" (1:55)—not a decoration. It was the essence of the individual and "la quintessence de toutes les vertus" (3:71). All this is very vague, and deliberately so, for the assumption was that the elite circle for whom these words were intended could reach behind the imprecision. The ideal was not accessible to all—in fact, was never meant to be—but rather had meaning for a certain few seeking to maintain, for themselves and the society that surrounded and observed them, their superior status. Méré was intent upon establishing a moral code, one to be deciphered by the maréchal de Clérambault and a few others, but clearly restricted in its accessibility. Nothing has really changed, the "essence" of nobility has remained

[18]

intact; but with the shift from ethical to aesthetic criteria, success may be more attainable, failure less traumatic.

*L'honnêteté* for the chevalier de Méré takes precedence over any rival demands, which explains why love, spontaneous and uncontrollable, finds little place in his moral universe. He believed that *l'honnêteté* was a complete moral system requiring total commitment: "La considération de ce qui est honnête, et de ce qui ne l'est pas, doit faire toute l'étude, et toute la conduite de notre vie" (*Réf.*, 7). A sharply penetrating and discerning mind was also necessary. Emphasis throughout Méré's works is on conscious, reasoned behavior; the passions must be kept in check: "Pour être sage, il faut que l'esprit et la raison soumettent le coeur, et pour être méchant, il faut que le coeur domine la raison et l'esprit" (*Réf.*, 262). Although this dichotomy is expressed in rather unsophisticated terms (and surely deliberately so)—the mind is "good," and the heart is "bad" —it does convey the chevalier's fundamental view of life. The spontaneous irrationality of passion is alien to his ideal, which, though not excluding love, nonetheless makes room only for an ascetic, untroubling *amour honnête*.

The preeminence of *l'honnêteté* is never in doubt. Portrayed as solid, durable, and eminently worthy in every way, the ideal contrasts with the evanescent passions:

> L'honnêteté se montre si agréable à toute sorte de jour, qu'elle mérite bien qu'on la cherche; et quand on la trouve, et qu'on ne la perd point de vue, on ne manque jamais de l'acquérir. Ayons-la toujours devant les yeux, et si nos passions nous veulent détourner de ce qu'elle nous ordonne, rebuttons-les sévèrement. . . . Nous y sentirons d'abord quelque contrainte, mais elle ne sera pas longue, et puis à considérer nos plus sensibles contentements, ils s'en vont bien vite, à peu près comme un songe agréable. (3:88)

The passions, and the pleasure they procure, are seen as a mere dream; *l'honnêteté* appears as an enduring, even permanent, force. The ephemeral quality that Méré accords to love refers not only to time. He perceives love as an illu-

[19]

sion when contrasted with the moral firmness of *l'hon-nêteté*.

The passions emerge in Méré's works as not only ephemeral but also debasing for man: "La raison distingue l'homme de l'animal, mais la passion le confond avec lui" (*Réf.*, 136). This traditional Christian view is further developed in one important letter, which Méré constructs as a conversation between himself and La Rochefoucauld. The conversation is probably apocryphal, and the ideas those of the chevalier alone. In any case, the letter confirms his belief that physical love is crude and impure, for he is in ready agreement with "La Rochefoucauld": "Je trouve aussi que ces plaisirs sensuels sont grossiers, sujets au dégoût et pas trop à rechercher, à moins que ceux de l'esprit ne s'y mêlent. Le plus sensible est celui de l'amour, mais il passe bien vite si l'esprit n'est de la partie" (*Let.*, 90). Yet another letter explains that physical love alone is morally unsatisfactory, adding that "lorsque les grâces de l'esprit et du bon air accompagnent la beauté du corps, l'amour n'a rien qui dégoûte" (*Let.*, 682).

For Méré the erotic impulse is also wild, uncontrolled, and unpredictable, offering distressing potential for individual alienation. Love contradicts reason and moderation —"La sagesse et l'amour ne s'accordent jamais" (*Réf.*, 143) —and is an inherently destructive force—"L'amour est semblable au feu, il brille et plaît quand on en est éloigné: mais il brûle et consume quand on s'en approche de trop près" (*Réf.*, 144). These reflections, though rather banal, set the tone for Méré's analysis. What concerns him is the disruptive nature of love, its capacity for estranging the "true" self. His fictional characters serve to illustrate this fear: "On aime Armide dans le camp des Chrétiens, parce qu'elle s'y présente douce et composée dans une grande modération, mais quand Renaud la quitte . . . et que dans l'excès de sa colère et de ses regrets elle ne garde plus de mesures, quelle différence d'elle à elle-même" (2:15)?

The "true" self as envisioned by the chevalier may be loosely described as the conscious, reasoning side of man.

Méré's efforts are directed toward dominating and controlling the unreasoning, subconscious layers of the self. His
writings frequently reflect an analytical naïveté so strong
for one of Méré's general perceptiveness that deliberate,
studied ignorance can be the only explanation: "Mais encore, comment se peut-il que l'amour et la haine se trouvent quelquefois à un si haut point dans un même coeur,
et qu'on puisse traiter si cruellement des personnes qu'on
aime d'un amour extrême" (*Let.*, 674)? This superficial
psychology contradicts the perceptions of other classical
writers, such as Racine, who explored fully the love-hate
dichotomy. Méré, however, categorically rejects what he
views as immoral behavior, and his rejection takes the form
of suspended belief.

He is blind also to other "anomalies" of love. In one
letter to a female correspondent, the chevalier ponders
how the superior traits associated with *l'honnêteté* can fail
to engender deep love: "La beauté, l'agrément, l'honnêteté, la bonne mine, les grâces du corps et de l'esprit, ce
sont des grands attraits pour se faire aimer; et nous voyons
néanmoins que ces belles qualités produisent bien souvent
un effet contraire, tant à l'égard des hommes que des
femmes" (*Let.*, 672). There follows a long list of "aberra-
tions," which appear to be both historical (Henri II and
the duchesse de Valentinois) and fictional ("un grand Seigneur fort bien fait, fort galant," who loved only physically
deformed men), and which illustrate the intensity of Méré's
stance.

It may be said also that the chevalier feared that love
could weaken the male. The *Réflexions morales* focus on
this question in some detail. To support the general statement "L'amour excite le courage quand il est dans la
modération, mais sitôt qu'il porte un homme jusque dans
la volupté, il le ramolit, bien loin de le rendre vigoureux"
(*Réf.*, 170), Méré offers in the following reflection several
classic examples of men rendered "soft" by women—Achilles
and Polyxena, Antony and Cleopatra. Thus, against a
*morale* of softness, irrationality, and alienation, Méré will

[21]

propose another vision, *l'honnêteté*, an ideal that point by point surpasses erotic love.

For not only is *l'honnêteté* durable, whereas passion is perceived as ephemeral, what further distinguishes the chevalier's goal is its capacity for engendering happiness:

> L'honnêteté me semble la chose du monde la plus aimable, et les personnes de bon sens ne mettent pas en doute, que nous ne la devons aimer, que parce qu'elle nous rend heureux: Car la félicité, comme on sait, est la dernière fin des choses, que nous entreprenons. Ainsi tout ce qui n'y contribue en rien, quoique l'on s'en imagine quelque apparence honnête, c'est toujours une fausse honnêteté. . . .
> Car à bien examiner toutes les vertus, elles ne sont pas à rechercher que de cela seulement, qu'elles peuvent servir à notre bonheur. (3:99)

Méré also emphasizes the relationship between *l'honnêteté* and happiness in his correspondence: "Tout ce qui ne peut contribuer à nous rendre la vie agréable, ce doit compter pour rien; l'honnêteté même qu'on estime tant, n'est à souhaiter que parce qu'elle rend heureux ceux qui l'ont et ceux qui l'approchent" (*Let.*, 318). Méré stresses happiness because he seeks to dismantle another ideal, *la vraie vertu*, that prevailed earlier in the century. Happiness was never the goal of *la vraie vertu*, which strove instead for loftiness and integrity even at the expense of life itself.

Unlike *l'honnêteté*, however, love is directly associated with suffering—"Qui commence à aimer, doit se préparer à souffrir" (*Réf.*, 138)—and with despair—"L'affection dégénère facilement en désespoir sitôt qu'elle n'a plus d'espérance; elle veut tout perdre, quand elle ne peut rien gagner" (*Réf.*, 137). Indeed, in those letters that appear free of the *galanteries* that color much of the correspondence, Méré is genuinely pained by love's disappointments:

> En effet je trouve que je m'engage extrêmement, et d'abord je ne croyais pas que cela dût aller si loin . . . j'avais bien quelque pressentiment que je courais plus de hasard auprès de vous que je n'avais fait partout ailleurs; mais parce que

j'avais vu beaucoup d'occasions où je m'étais sauvé des plus grands dangers sans blessure ou du moins sans blessure mortelle, je me fiais trop à ma fortune, et pour dire le vrai, j'étais bien imprudent de ne pas craindre d'être si souvent tête-à-tête avec vous dans les Tuileries. (*Let.*, 171–72)

It is not the intention here to explore Méré's motivations, and the above passage may or may not express genuine emotional anguish. Whether the words are "sincere" is not germane, for, in any case, they correspond perfectly to the general tenor of Méré's writings: love is associated with emotional wounds, with suffering, and is rarely the beneficiary of the "positive thinking" reserved for *l'honnêteté*.

There is, however, yet one more important characteristic of *l'honnêteté*: the quest for aesthetic perfection. This artistic element sharply distinguishes Méré's ideal from the naturalness of love. Critics have detected an artificial quality to *l'honnêteté*, as formulated by the chevalier; but significantly, the artificial in his works is linked closely with art. Theater metaphors are prominent, frequently in relation to the chevalier's ideal man: "Le personnage d'un honnête homme s'étend partout; il se doit transformer par la souplesse du génie, comme l'occasion le demande" (3:157). Méré thinks in terms of audiences, of society as a "watching" public. Thus his *honnête homme* must never fail to captivate and seduce.

In what may seem initially paradoxical, and in contradiction to the artistic imagery, Méré portrays *l'honnête homme* as a completely natural figure. His person must be unaffected and unadorned. For *l'honnête femme*, makeup and fancy dress are rejected as masks of the natural self. Pedantry is attacked as a cover-up for true knowledge, as is brilliance that lacks depth:

Mais les gens faits, et qui jugent bien, n'aiment pas les choses de montre, et qui parent beaucoup, quand elles ne sont que de peu de valeur. Celles qui n'ont guère d'éclat,

et qui sont de grand prix, leur plaisent. Cela se remarque
en tout, et même en ce qui concerne l'esprit et les pensées.
Car si ces sortes de choses semblent fort belles, et qu'elles
ne soient belles qu'en apparence, elles dégoûtent tout aus-
sitôt, et celles qui le sont sans le paraître, plus on les considère, plus on les trouve à son gré. C'est qu'elles sont belles
sans être parées, et qu'on y découvre de temps en temps
des grâces secrètes, qu'on n'avait pas aperçues. (1:56)

Méré had a penchant for all in life that is secret, undetected,
below the surface. "Ces beautés secrètes" form an integral
part of his aesthetics, contrasting with the seduction of surface attractions.

The natural state of things, however, is not always
sufficiently commanding. The superior individual—male or
female—must strive for perfection, and it is in this effort
that the artistic goal is realized: "Sans mentir," writes
Méré to one correspondent, "vous avez eu jusqu'ici trop
de confiance aux avantages que la nature vous a donnés:
et puisque vous voulez que je vous éclaircisse de tout,
sachez que le plus beau naturel est peu de chose à moins
qu'on n'ait soin de le perfectionner" (*Let.*, 502). Social
man is viewed here as a living work of art, whence the
appropriateness of aesthetic standards.

The artistic ideal does not function in a vacuum. Aesthetic perfection is not only an aspect of courtly conduct.
For Méré *l'honnêteté* continually transcended limited notions of aristocratic man at court. If he dwells extensively
on aesthetic perfection, it is in large part because of association with the theme of control. *L'honnête homme* thus
becomes a highly complex figure, whose essential posture
of sharp observation combined with a possessing style
leads to complete domination over his audience: "Nous
avons toujours quelque chose qui nous tient au coeur, et
nous touche sensiblement: et c'est un grand avantage, que
de pénétrer ce faible pour gagner les personnes comme on
veut" (3:152).

The type of control he envisions, however, is of a special
nature. Domination for Méré means seduction, in both

the broadest connotation and the most sexually limited one. It is, moreover, in the art of language that the chevalier finds the most satisfactory means to successful "penetration," hence, to control. His letters, as well as the conversations with the maréchal de Clérambault, emphasize that perfection in eloquence is the way to success, whereas the "right" language is also judged essential in the art of sexual seduction. In both cases aesthetic domination of an audience is the primary goal.

As a strictly social concept, free of sexual orientation, Méré's art consists of winning over others through elegant discourse: "Quand on s'est acquis toutes les qualités qu'on peut souhaiter pour être éloquent, on est assuré de plaire et de persuader, et même de se faire admirer dans tous les sujets agréables" (*Let.*, 371-72). It is significant that the art of pleasing is coupled here with the art of persuasion. *L'art de plaire* is the basis of Méré's ideal, but the connotations are complex. *L'honnêteté* transcends the ideas of "pleasing" associated with gallant behavior and relies upon an aesthetically defined social presence in order to achieve total domination: "Mais je vous puis assurer que l'on ne saurait trop avoir une certaine justesse de langage, qui consiste à se servir des meilleures façons de parler, pour mettre sa pensée dans l'esprit des gens comme on veut qu'elle y soit, ni plus ni moins" (1:15). Elegance and refinement are not meant only to "please"; they are also, perhaps principally for Méré, a sure means to molding and controlling others' thinking.

When domination is sexualized, skillful use of language is equally essential. In the *Conversations* Méré shows how indulging in verbal excesses and failing to control language can ruin a suitor's attempt to please and seduce: "On leur [les femmes] jette son coeur à la tête, et d'abord on leur en dit plus que la vraisemblance ne leur permet d'en croire, et bien souvent plus qu'elles n'en veulent" (1:21). Although Méré explains that seduction of women involves diverse "agréments," he places particular stress on verbal art. Contrasting Caesar in battle to Caesar seducing Cleopatra, the chevalier highlights two diverging means for success, but which are equally dependent upon appropriate expression and style.

By far the richest example, however, of the adroit use of language in the art of seduction is detailed in a letter where Méré purports to relate a "friend's" adventures. In this situation a would-be lover, disguised as a family tutor, successfully gains the complete attention of the woman he desires. His method is unusual—mastery of the art of reading aloud—but destined to succeed:

> Il faut donc que je tâche de lui plaire en tirant la quintessence de tous les agréments qui la peuvent toucher par la meilleure manière de lire; elle consiste à bien prononcer les mots, et d'un ton conforme au sujet du discours, que ma parole la flatte sans l'endormir, qu'elle l'éveille sans la choquer, que j'use d'inflexions pour ne la pas lasser, que je prononce tendrement et d'une voix mourante les choses tendres; mais d'une façon si tempérée qu'elle n'y sente rien d'affecté. Je fis en peu de jours tant de progrès en cette étude qu'elle ne se plaisait plus qu'à me faire lire et qu'à s'entretenir avec moi. (*Let.*, 60)

Here Méré portrays the erotic domination of an audience through close attention to subtleties of style and form. Perfected, artificial expression replaces natural conversation as a first important step in seducing the woman. It is surely not coincidental that the language Méré's "friend" adopts to recount his little tale is charged with a latent sensuality ("je prononce tendrement et d'une voix mourante les choses tendres"), which communicates the desired goal of seduction. Thus if verbal excess may lead to failure in seducing a woman, careful attention to language may, on the other hand, engender considerable success. The veracity of the above story is of little consequence. Hyperbole may well have come into play. But even if Méré has exaggerated the role of polished language arts, the story still conveys an idea essential to his thinking: the erotic domination of an audience through an aesthetic medium.

What Méré develops is a desexualized portrait of love,

for diverse reasons. There is surely an Epicurean element to his works. In their descriptions of the ideal woman, the Epicureans emphasized both physical charm and a high degree of intelligence. Many passages in the chevalier's works allude to the importance of intellectual ability in women, and the stress that he places on this talent results, in part, from an attitude that values intelligent discourse. "Ce qui fait principalement que vous plaisez toujours," writes Méré to a female correspondent, "c'est que vous avez l'esprit fin, avec une extrême justesse à parler, à vous taire, à être douce ou fière, enjouée ou sérieuse, et à prendre dans les moindres choses que vous dites le meilleur ton et le meilleur tour" (2:10).

But if Méré's philosophical ties to Epicureanism are always apparent, they do not sufficiently explain the formulation of his ideal. Maurice Magendie believes that the *mondain* code, which banished spontaneity and relied heavily upon convention, may have been a reaction against "la sensualité sans esprit mise à la mode par le Vert Galant."[4] Méré's strong sense of refinement, his quest for the correct airs, and his close attention to style, and particularly to style in language, do indeed offer an alternative to overemphasis on sensuality. As such, *l'honnêteté* becomes a form of sublimation.

Perhaps there is another reason, related to the above but sufficiently distinct to warrant mentioning. "La galanterie," one critic has written, "est un alibi commode. Elle introduit dans la conversation entre hommes et femmes un langage qui, malgré ses conventions, reste un langage amoureux . . . c'est le chemin naturel de la séduction."[5] Many of Méré's letters to female friends testify to a highly cultivated form of *galanterie*. (This impression, impossible to prove, results from the cumulative effect of reading a large number of very similar letters to women correspondents.) What the letters, essays, and dialogues convey is that attention to style and language has become a means to achieving emotional independence while still ensuring the success of the game of love.

Both Magendie and Duchêne offer meaningful explanations of Méré's goal—the de-sensualizing of love in favor of an aesthetically defined *art de plaire*. Méré does incorporate an ethical standard into his writings. By stating that "il est certain que quand on aime une personne d'un mérite exquis, cet amour remplit d'honnêteté le coeur et l'esprit et donne toujours de plus nobles pensées, que l'affection qu'on a pour une personne ordinaire" (2:81), the chevalier suggests that his ideal is morally superior. But despite the introduction of this ethical standard, Méré still conveyes a socialized view of love. As the above passage suggests, love is a means for arriving at the perfection of the self that Méré calls *l'honnêteté*. "C'est de l'amour, que naissent la plupart des vrais agréments" (3:75). This cause-and-effect relation communicates the diminished stress on individual feeling and the heightened stature of pleasability that are the mark of the chevalier de Méré's works. Within his moral universe, there is little room for the solipsistic spontaneity and intensity of passion. At best, reciprocal *honnêteté* has become the ideal in a world where social perfection is the highest standard.

1. Antoine Gombaud, chevalier de Méré, *Oeuvres complètes*, ed. Charles-H. Boudhors (Paris: Editions Fernand Roches, 1930); *Maximes, sentences et réflexions morales et politiques* (Paris: 1687); *Lettres* (Paris: 1689). Subsequent references to Méré's works will appear in the text. For the *Oeuvres complètes* (which include the *Conversations* and the *Discours*) both volume and page number will be given; the *Maximes, sentences et réflexions morales et politiques* will be abbreviated as *Réf.*, and the entry number will appear as the reference; for the *Lettres* the page number will be given.

2. Edmond Chamaillard, *Le Chevalier de Méré, suivi d'un choix de lettres et de pensées du Chevalier* (Paris: G. Clouzot, 1921), p. 81.

3. Jean Starobinski, "La Rochefoucauld et les morales substitutives," *Nouvelle revue française* 14 (August 1966): 211.

4. Maurice Magendie, *La Politesse mondaine et les théories de l'honnêteté en France au XVIIᵉ siècle, de 1600 à 1660*, 2 vols. in 1 (Geneva: Slatkine Reprints, 1970), 1:133.

5. Roger Duchêne, *Réalité vécue et art épistolaire: Madame de Sévigné et la lettre d'amour* (Paris: Bordas, 1970), p. 53.

Chapter Two

## LA ROCHEFOUCAULD

THE *MAXIMES* TOTALLY DEFY critical discourse as we know it; their fragmented structure is at variance with a continuous, organized flow of words. And yet the temptation to order, to structure, to systematize, remains strong, almost as if the fragmentary form provoked some special challenge. Hypotheses explaining why La Rochefoucauld favored the maxim have been amply formulated, perhaps most satisfactorily by Jean Starobinski,[1] for whom the maxim corresponds to the demands of a subject matter imbued with a sense of man's physical and psychic "fragmentation." But even—or perhaps especially—the most perceptive analysis is in radical contradiction with the work as La Rochefoucauld presented it, for a continuous, structured chapter or essay brings to the *Maximes* the very sense of order that the author clearly sought to avoid.

It is perhaps our ambiguous, uncomfortable relationship to the *discontinu* in literature that lies at the base of any effort to link what was so deliberately left unjoined. (This discomfort was not experienced, of course, in the classical age, heir to a long tradition in the aesthetics of the *discontinu*, from the *Odyssey* up through Montaigne. Rather, our own reactions emanate from the university criticism of the nineteenth century and its efforts to impose rigor and structure.) As Roland Barthes has shown in his essay "Littérature et discontinu," modern Western thought will accept, at best, only certain specific forms of the discontinuous: "Le livre discontinu n'est toléré que dans ses emplois bien réservés: soit comme recueil de fragments (Héraclite, Pascal), le caractère *inachevé* de l'oeuvre (mais s'agit-il au fond d'oeuvres inachevées?) corroborant en somme *a contrario* l'excellence du continu, hors duquel il y a quelquefois ébauche, mais jamais perfection; soit comme recueil d'aphorismes, car l'aphorisme est un petit continu tout plein, l'affirmation théâtrale que le vide est horrible."[2] La Rochefoucauld's *Maximes*, although not exactly proverbial, belong certainly both in *forme* and *fond* to a tradition of pithy, moral reflection. Nevertheless, a certain malaise remains; there is a desire, a need, to connect.

Because the adage or maxim is its own entity, inevitably any attempt to agglomerate falsifies its basic premise of structural independence. The whole becomes equal to the sum of its parts; but it may well be that any "adding up" process is irreconcilable with intention. Nonetheless, once the critic decides to comment upon the text, he has no other choice than to structure into an intelligible whole the sum total of the *Maximes* (selecting certain ones as representative of other similar maxims), or, on a more-reduced plane, to study one aspect (theme) of the work, again organizing the individual parts into a new, larger entity— virtue, *amour-propre*, and so on. The sole alternative possibility is to comment on each individual maxim, with no attempt made to relate it to any others. But this seems to be an unnecessary task, the success of the *Maximes* being due precisely to their polished form, which gives the "truth" in a more formally perfect fashion than any equivalent expression.

The outcome of this enterprise is necessarily a certain gap between text and critical text. Ultimately, the *Maximes* taken as a whole are impenetrable. Their fragmentation, their sense of indivisible totality, escape any notion of system. Nevertheless, this section is an attempt at "penetrating" the maxims that revolve about the theme of love, although an overly rigid systematization will be carefully shunned.

But once the project is stated and accepted, other problems immediately arise within the bounds of the topic itself. La Rochefoucauld's pronouncements on love resist almost any categorizing, however fluid. In the *Maximes* alone, he moves from one "mode" of love to another, runs the gamut between *la coquetterie* and a nebulous nostalgia for a "pure" love, remote, abstract, unattainable. And only recently an additional important manuscript has been added to the works of La Rochefoucauld, *La Justification de l'amour*, whose heavy emphasis on *la courtoisie* seems to be in contradiction with the basic tenets of the *Maximes*.[3] Synthesis becomes a near impossibility. But one basic underlying concept does seem to blend the diverse, even sometimes diverging, ideas together—the notion of a passive man, a receptacle for an ever present flow of *impulsions*, an individual whose very autonomy seems little more than illusory.

Traditionally, *l'amour-propre* has been seized upon as the fundamental current of the *Maximes*, the irreducible unit to which all of human thought and deed eventually succumb. The familiar paradigm unfolds as a dialectic between diverse outer manifestations and one basic inner motivation, *l'amour-propre*. However, in a series of articles begun in 1962 and concluded in 1966, Jean Starobinski reverses this premise, which has long held sway. Relying upon certain maxims that center upon inner division, split, rather than on motivating unity, Starobinski concludes that the so-called external chaos is infinitely more simple than that which reigns "underneath."[4] Maxim 16 (of the 1678 edition) offers, for example, a multiplicity of motivations to explain clemency: "Cette clémence dont on fait une vertu se pratique tantôt par vanité, quelquefois par paresse, souvent par crainte, et presque toujours par tous les trois ensemble."[5] Causation reveals itself as both complex and flexible.

Delving further, Starobinski dissociates the "self" from

*l'amour-propre*, showing that the two are not equivalent for La Rochefoucauld, and that *l'amour-propre* is only one *impulsion* that appropriates the self. The latter emerges as an empty, hollow space, a vacuum, subject to invasion not only by self-love but by all forces. Vice, virtue, passion, all are conceived as "outside" of man, exterior to him, almost as floating energies.[6] Starobinski's theory is substantiated by a careful reading of the *Maximes*. What strikes immediately is La Rochefoucauld's frequent use of personification, this literary device being not only a colorful stylistic variation but rather the means by which the maxim-writer expresses the very tension integral to his work. When La Rochefoucauld writes that "l'amour-propre est le plus grand de tous les flatteurs" (*Max.* 2) or that "l'amour-propre est plus habile que le plus habile homme du monde" (*Max.* 4), he is endowing self-love with qualities of functioning independence and virtual autonomy, rivaling man's own and therefore a threat to the philosophical beliefs of voluntarism and freedom that he cherishes. Various maxims establish structures parallel to, and competing with, man's own "systems": "Les passions ont une injustice et un propre intérêt qui fait qu'il est dangereux de les suivre . . . " (*Max.* 9). Not only is mankind endowed with an unmitigating self-interest, but so also are the intruding passions, their foundation a twin of the individual's. Those scholars who seek to determine the precise philosophical bent of the *Maximes* have justifiably concentrated on their antistoical posture, and the constant use of personification to depict man's loss of autonomy, his fall from the grace of voluntarism, is the perfect image of the new thinking.

As tempting, then, as it is to view *l'amour* as an interrupting force into the privileged domain of *l'amour-propre*, this perspective simply does not hold up. In fact, if a schematization is necessary at all, it would have to be one that depicts love and self-love as two parallel forces, each making its independent set of demands upon the vacuum of the self. That La Rochefoucauld conceived of these forces as operating in similar fashion, is reflected in his choice of imagery. Both the long digression on *l'amour-propre* and one of the *Réflexions diverses*, "De l'amour et de la mer," use the metaphor of the sea to translate the sense of movement and flow with which he endows both energies.

There is considerably more to be said on the question of movement and energy, central to La Rochefoucauld's thinking and most prevalent throughout the *Maximes* and his other works. But this thinking is seemingly at variance, or at least does not obviously correlate, with his views on love as he expressed them in 1660, when *La Justification de l'amour* first appeared, a date that corresponds to the writing of the earliest maxims. The subtleties, nuances, and paradoxes of the *Maximes* and of a few of the *Réflexions diverses* are absent from the *Justification*, which at preliminary reading fails to convince the reader that the work is indeed one of La Rochefoucauld's. Or at best the text seems to be a *plaidoyer*, urging a woman to quit her modesty and to bestow her favors upon the author.[7] But although this last possibility may not be totally false, ultimately the *Justification* does seem to offer several parallels with the *Maximes* and with a few of the longer pieces.

Since the publication of *La Justification de l'amour* is quite recent (1971), some preliminary background information is necessary:

> *La Justification de l'amour* parut au début de 1660—l'achevé d'imprimer date du 13 décembre 1659—dans le troisième volume du *Recueil des pièces en prose les plus agréables de ce temps* chez Charles de Sercy. Ce traité, qui se divise en trois parties, occupe les pages 289 à 334, précédant ainsi un texte bien connu de La Rochefoucauld, *L'Amour-propre à Mademoiselle*, qui va jusqu'à la page 344. Bien sûr, une telle juxtaposition dans un recueil collectif ne prouve rien en lui-même. Mais cet indice prend une certaine importance du fait que Sercy cherchait à grouper les pièces par auteurs. (P. 10)

My analysis, though not able to ascertain positively that the *Justification* is by La Rochefoucauld, does try to involve

[33]

it in the larger group of his known works. In any case (as with the "Pascalian" *Discours sur les passions de l'amour*), even if the work is not by the author of the *Maximes*, it nevertheless belongs to an analogous group of writings and therefore reflects their concerns and expression. For my purposes, I will here consider the work as one of La Rochefoucauld's, although I am aware of, and accept as potentially valid, the questions concerning the authenticity.

What is significant is that the date of publication of the treatise on love corresponds approximately to the composition of the earliest maxims. Therefore, it would be false to attempt a study of the evolution of La Rochefoucauld's ideas on love when, in fact, many of his most important views seem to have evolved during the same period. In some ways this makes the task more difficult. There is no means to establish any transition in his thought, and the concordance of dates would seem to suggest that very possibly two different forces were in operation at the same moment: "une réhabilitation de l'amour et une contestation de tous les grands sentiments de l'homme" (pp. 16-17).

Basically, both the *Maximes* and *La Justification de l'amour* originate in the same metaphysical source: man is subject to "invasion" by exterior forces and energies. The personification so prevalent throughout the *Maximes*—the stylistic device by which La Rochefoucauld was best able to translate his view of man's place in the world—appears also in the treatise on love, although in a somewhat different vein. In both works man is struggling, at war with (martial metaphors appear throughout the apology of love), outside elements, his autonomy is called into question, and he is drawn as a passive agent in a world of forces over which he has little control. But whereas there is no resolution to this confrontation in the *Maximes*, only a full acknowledgment of the chaos inherent in love, as well as recognition of its inevitable, sad end, in the *Justification* the weakness of the male lover becomes the means to establishing a stable situation where love can exist, as a secret.

The deterministic view of man and the passions is as fully expressed in the *Justification* as in the *Maximes*,[8] but the

[34]

images coincide perfectly with the general *courtois, précieux* tone: "L'Amour, ce dit Platon, est un puissant Magicien, qui attire soudainement les coeurs, et transforme étrangement les volontés. La beauté que ce Sexe adorable possède par éminence, et avec exclusion du nôtre, est le premier philtre duquel l'Amour se sert pour cet effet" (pp. 38-39). The reference to the philter, to the magic potion with all its ties to legend, is more than simple *courtois* vocabulary. If love is a magic potion, man is the passive agent who drinks from it, and immediately, all notions of responsibility disappear. Drinking the love philter has long been an ideal way to communicate abnegation of human freedom dependent upon choice, and to enhance a sense of mutual, although involuntary, obligation. The entire concept of a floating love-energy, a "potion" distinct from the self, that the individual absorbs into his system does not at all betray La Rochefoucauld's views on the invasion by annihilating *impulsions*, but rather reflects the deterministic bent of his thinking.

The personification so evident in the *Maximes* is given an enhanced status in the treatise on love, where it borders on allegory. The use of capital letters for "Amour" and "Beauté" provides them with a sense of independence, as they seduce and ensnare man. "Beauty" is furnished with supreme power (although in a traditional Epicurean vein, the mind also participates in the all-encompassing attraction), at war with man's so-called indomitable nature:

> La Beauté, cette chose admirable dont l'on sent la puissance bien plus facilement que l'on n'en explique la nature; ce rayon de la Divinité; cette Reine victorieuse des Sages les plus modérés, et des Conquérants les plus invincibles; cette qualité dont la domination est si bien établie, qu'encore que toutes les Créatures semblent être armées pour la combattre. . . . Enfin cette Beauté peut-elle trouver un coeur qui lui fasse une opiniâtre résistance? (Pp. 40-41)

The passage is written in the over-refined, over-elegant style of the *Précieuses*, and adheres to the *courtois* code. Nevertheless, the personification, the quasi-allegorical note,

[35]

follow perfectly La Rochefoucauld's fundamental beliefs. The warlike metaphors additionally support the view of man as being intruded upon, invaded by potent energies, "determined" by them. Everything has become an "actor" on the world's stage, rivaling for possession of the self. "Le 'conflit des passions'—dramaturgie figurée, psychomachie allégorique—se fait passer pour la réalité dernière et pour le sens véridique de la vie intérieure."[9] However, the belief that man is not responsible for his desire is mediated in the *Justification*, where emotional bondage is viewed as pleasurable. In the essay on love, man is portrayed as the adoring slave to woman; in the *Maximes*, on the other hand, he is depicted as bound by love, an imperfect, debilitating, and autocratic force.

Personification is not the sole link between the two works. The concept of *le vrai amour* appears throughout both the treatise and the aphorisms. Although the latter focus on love as an imperfect force, quick to dissipate into coquetry, gallantry, or total stagnation, there is nevertheless room in the *Maximes* for an ideal love: "S'il y a un amour pur et exempt du mélange de nos autres passions, c'est celui qui est caché au fond du coeur, et que nous ignorons nous-mêmes" (*Max.* 69). Similarly, in the opening section of the *Justification*, La Rochefoucauld quickly establishes what love is not: "L'Amour est le nom du monde le plus commun, et la chose la plus rare: tout le monde en parle; beaucoup de personnes croient le ressentir; peu le connaissent; et cette ignorance produit . . . tant de fausses galanteries qui sont si ordinaires, et lesquelles sont plutôt contraires à l'Amour, qu'elles n'en sont les effets" (pp. 27-28). In both works La Rochefoucauld carefully distinguishes between the commonplace reality and the exceptional ideal. "Il semble donc," concludes Hubert, "qu'il ait vu dans chaque vertu et dans chaque passion avouable de l'homme un cas limite, un état exceptionnel, qu'il faudrait à tout prix atteindre sous peine de s'enliser dans ce monde équivoque où les vertus sont des vices déguisés et où l'amour se confond avec la vanité" (p. 19).

[36]

The presentation of *le vrai amour*, however, is not parallel in the two works. In the *Maximes* it is maintained as a remote ideal, a goal that man will never attain. Perfect love in the *Justification*, on the other hand, though still idealistically portrayed, is a real possibility for mankind, if not for all men, then at least for an elite circle of *honnêtes gens*. *L'honnêteté* is not a predominant theme of the *Maximes*, although it does figure in the *Réflexions diverses*. However, in *La Justification de l'amour*, La Rochefoucauld focuses on *l'honnêteté*, establishing a strong tie between that superior moral ideal and love.

In the opening part of the essay, the moralist openly justifies love to its critics—"le vrai Amour est la chose du monde la plus raisonnable" (p. 30)—and in the best Epicurean tradition paints a harmonious picture of attraction based equally on feminine beauty and merit. (The work, it should be made clear, is written exclusively from a male point of view, although La Rochefoucauld does distinguish between male and female reactions in matters of love.) It is, however, at the end of the first section and throughout the second that La Rochefoucauld develops his most original and, for this study, most significant ideas, particularly in his analysis of the secret.

In the introduction to *La Justification de l'amour*, Hubert maintains that the close attention La Rochefoucauld accords secret love is the strongest reason for attributing the essay to the author of the *Maximes*. The latter work does emphasize hidden, secret elements in man's moral life. But if the two works utilize a common principle, they do not pursue the idea along parallel lines. The term *cacher* assumes two very different connotations.

"Qui aime, et ne témoigne pas la Passion à l'objet de son Amour si adroitement, et par des moyens si respectueux, qu'elle ne s'en puisse abstenir, est timide, et manque à l'Amour même. Qui n'a pas assez de conduite pour cacher sa Passion à toutes les autres personnes, en la faisant connaître à la seule qu'il aime, est peu judicieux, et n'aime pas bien" (p. 62). Love, then, is to remain a complete secret from the world. For transmitting the passion to the "love object," such communication may utilize only the most respectful means. These methods, as the second section will inform, are rarely verbal, or verbal only in the final stages. La Rochefoucauld has developed a theory that first isolates love, removing it from the eyes of the world, then tames it to such a degree that to "talk love" is itself a "sin," violating the rather ascetic criteria of merit and esteem (key principles of *l'honnêteté*) that tolerate only a discreet sign language.

This is not to say that language is not important in the art of wooing. In *La Justification de l'amour*, it is essential, but in a limited context:

> Il nous ordonne de commencer la conduite de notre Passion par une connaissance la plus parfaite que nous puissions tirer de la personne que nous aimons, et particulièrement les sentiments qu'elle a en général touchant l'Amour; d'essayer de lui témoigner en toutes rencontres une extrême curiosité de savoir les pensées qu'elle peut avoir sur ce sujet; de renouveler autant que la licence le permet les discours qui touchent cette matière. (P. 64)

In a note to the above passage, J. D. Hubert remarks that the art of loving expressed here resembles closely the art of conversation as developed in the *Réflexions diverses*: "On ne saurait avoir trop d'application à connaître la pente et la portée de ceux à qui on parle . . ." (p. 192). The point is significant and deserves further analysis. As in the writings of the chevalier de Méré, the *Justification* socializes love. This is not to say that the essay involves the lover in a large context: he is, to the contrary, isolated, refused the pleasure of divulging his feelings. However, in describing love in terms that bear a close resemblance to the art of conversation, La Rochefoucauld stresses not spontaneously experienced emotion but rather the controlled refinement of genteel society.

The second section, however, is less concerned with the couple than with the lover and the world, and the ban against communication is severe. No third party may share in the knowledge of the passion, which must remain an eternal secret: "Peut-être s'étonnera-t-on que la Loi de l'Amour, que l'on peut appeler la première, puisque c'est elle qui règle ses commandements, soit un commandement de le tenir couvert" (p. 68). The *précieux* tone of such "commandments" does not detract from an awareness that the interdiction against discussing or sharing the passion is absolute.

The final section of *La Justification* ("Suite de la seconde partie du traité de l'amour") develops and amplifies the themes of the earlier parts, with the taboo against language assuming greater force. It is no longer a question of maintaining a secret, but of how to communicate with the female. Forthright avowal of love may occur, but only if explicitly permitted by the woman, and only after the acceptance by her of other signs, judged less demeaning to the *morale* of *l'honnêteté*. The spoken word itself is seen as a transgression, no less threatening than a physical act. In this context, where gesture and action are never even brought into question, to speak of love is the ultimate violation. Speech must therefore be repressed by *l'honnête homme*—"Quelquefois il se considère soi-même dans un si grand, et si véritable excès de Passion, que sa grandeur lui donne de l'audace. En ce moment l'impatience de faire connaître ouvertement son Amour, lui porte la parole sur les lèvres; en celui-ci le respect la rejette dessus la langue" (p. 73)—as a means to tempering the passion and to maintaining the standards of esteem and respect.

The final pages of *La Justification de l'amour* focus almost exclusively on the question of language, as the author searches for more discreet methods of communication. There is an oblique element to these efforts, a desire to remain within the prescribed boundaries of *l'honnêteté*, even if only partial understanding results:

Je confesse que comme la sujétion entière de notre entendement à la personne que nous aimons est la marque la

[39]

plus particulière de la Passion que nous aurons pour elle, puisque nous la refusons même très souvent à nos Rois les plus légitimes, et que c'est l'unique service auquel les plus puissants Monarques de la Terre ne nous peuvent obliger, il est raisonnable que nous soyons extrêmement exacts à ne rendre point nos paroles criminelles, lesquelles sont les plus vives images de cet entendement. Je crois même que nous ne devons laisser jamais sortir de notre bouche ce mot, lequel étant permis nous donne tant de joie, et défendu nous charge de peines et de tourments, *je vous aime*, que nous n'ayons lu dans les yeux de celle à qui nous parlons, qu'elle a quelque pitié de notre mal; ou bien si nous ne sommes pas assez heureux pour tirer ce sentiment de son coeur, que la violence de nos souffrances ne rompe ce silence parlant. (Pp. 75-76)

Within the confines of *l'honnêteté*, "ultimate sin" has become the violation of specific language codes—"à ne rendre point nos paroles criminelles"—whose basis is decidedly non-erotic.

La Rochefoucauld does indicate that the woman may see fit to allow the potentially "criminal" words to be pronounced. The *précieux* tone of this earnestly expressed hope contrasts with the severity directed toward unencouraged love talk, conveying an emotional freedom on the part of the author. Unquestionably, the entire work is colored by elements of *la courtoisie* and *la préciosité*; and, in fact, the interdiction against direct avowal of love may be viewed as a conscious attempt by La Rochefoucauld to adhere to those traditions, particularly as regards the question of esteem. Through suppressing direct violations to the *précieux* tenets, the author may better persuade a woman, if that is his intention.

Nonetheless, the moralist's close, intense attention to language may also be viewed as an effort toward moderating potential disruption to the *morale* of *l'honnêteté*, itself antithetical to unbridled, spontaneous emotion. Direct avowal of passion is permissable only when other, less-threatening signs (particularly eye "language") have been received positively. Reliance on such non-verbal signs moderates what is otherwise perceived as a certain violation of social and moral dicta. In this context *l'amour honnête* coincides with *la préciosité*, with both attempting to circumvent the realities of passion through non-verbal means. The expression of love becomes then metaphoric.

The *Justification* is, in the end, an ambiguous work, professing to explain and justify love, yet fixed into an ascetic mold, where love is a secret from the world and, as regards the couple, a discreet, non-assertive sentiment controlled by the woman. There is surely a source of pleasure in the submissive, secretive stance of the lover, but such pleasure, consistently passive, is never the true focus of the essay. The thrust of the work is Epicurean, even Platonic at times, but beyond the philosophical base is the careful attention to regulating language in love matters. To control language is to control the passion itself, first separating it from the outside world into the domain of the secret, then moderating its expression to conform to the ascetic limits of *l'amour honnête*.

The *Justification* succeeds in harmonizing *l'amour-passion* with the behavior of *l'honnête homme*; *le vrai amour* remains an ideal throughout the work, but one that is portrayed as viable for an elite group of lovers, if only for them. The mood of the work is subdued, and love never finds expression in the *Justification*—either in the author's description or recommendations—beyond the levels dictated by social demands. Nevertheless, the effort, however diminished, is a positive one when contrasted with the *Maximes*, where no such resolution is offered. Love is seized upon, examined from every side, squeezed out, and left limply hanging. The harmonizing activities of the *Justification* and of certain of the *Réflexions diverses* are absent, and the sense of total determinism, no longer couched in the elegant phrases of the *courtois-précieux* mold, appears as a far more bitter pill. Moreover, the *vrai amour* is placed so far away from us that we are tantalized without receiving any hope of realization. As for the love we are allowed in our life, when it manages to exceed the boundaries of

[41]

coquetry and gallantry (a rare enough occurrence), it still, inevitably, ends and dies, and we are left with a sense of shame and an exhausted heart.

The deterministic view of life that ruled over *La Justification de l'amour* is, as I showed earlier, present throughout the maxims. But the aphorisms present a more complex view. "Reading through the *Maximes* consecutively, one may be struck by two evidently divergent principles of causal explanation. On the one hand, persistent attention to egotism and passion points to a far-reaching psychological determinism; on the other hand, emphasis upon fortune and the bodily humors as indomitable influences suggests an equally powerful physical determinism."[10] This dialectic is not really ever resolved in the *Maximes*, although, as Philip Lewis has shown, the maxim on *l'amour-propre*, which was number one in the first edition of the work but which La Rochefoucald later rejected, is able to link the ego's demands with forces from the outside: "Il [l'amour-propre] est inconstant, et outre les changements qui viennent des causes étrangères, il y en a une infinité qui naissent de lui, et de son propre fonds."[11] Nevertheless, the problem remains when individual maxims confront others of a different persuasion.

Maxim 262 of the 1678 edition, for example, states, "Il n'y a point de passion où l'amour de soi-même règne si puissamment que dans l'amour"; and Maxim 374 concludes, "Si on croit aimer sa maîtresse pour l'amour d'elle, on est bien trompé," the implication being, of course, that it is "pour l'amour de soi." Maxims such as these do indeed indicate a psychological base where *l'amour-propre* is seen as the major determining force behind man's love. In these cases, actually, "love" as we traditionally formulate it— as a reaching out to another—is stripped of that very implication. The "other" is present, but it is self-love that is ultimately at stake. This view is most nearly consistent with certain modern psychoanalytical ideas that center upon the theory of narcissism, holding that "love of self is of the same nature as love of another person, or of ex-

[42]

terior objects. Both are classified as sexual instincts and considered to originate in the libido."[12]

But in establishing priority, primary consideration should be given to external physical causes,[13] although La Rochefoucauld, fearing perhaps the consequence of stressing this attack on man's autonomy and will, omitted several maxims to that effect from the 1678 edition. (Most, in fact, were taken out after the publication of the first edition.) Frequently they are also the strongest thrusts against the prerogatives of the self, although a few significant maxims do remain in the established edition: "La durée de nos passions ne dépend pas plus de nous que la durée de notre vie" (*Max.* 5); "La fortune et l'humeur gouvernent le monde" (*Max.* 435).

It is, however, in the *maximes supprimées* that La Rochefoucauld develops the greatest indictment against freedom and will; and although the basic belief of causation is not very different from that expressed in the *Justification*, the language is far more acerbic. It is no longer a question of magicians and potions; the entire *précieux* tone has vanished, replaced by the metaphor of illness: "La plus juste comparaison qu'on puisse faire de l'amour, c'est celle de la fièvre; nous n'avons non plus de pouvoir sur l'un que sur l'autre, soit pour sa violence ou pour sa durée" (*Max. supp.* 59).[14] The conclusion is inevitable: "Comme on n'est jamais en liberté d'aimer, ou de cesser d'aimer, l'amant ne peut se plaindre avec justice de l'inconstance de sa maîtresse, ni elle de la légèreté de son amant" (*Max. supp.* 62). Love is not willed, nor will. And as Starobinski concludes: "L'homme est ainsi dépossédé. Il ne désire pas en personne, il n'est plus responsable de son désir. C'est le désir qui, venu on ne sait d'où, s'installe en l'homme et réclame satisfaction."[15]

Beyond the level of determinism, of erosion of autonomy, the *Maximes* take a quite different bent from the *Justification*. The greatest concentration of thought on the theme of love in the maxims is directed toward the dynamics of Eros, both the internal movement necessary to maintain its force as well as the cyclical flow of passion. Prone to a certain amount of concrete imagery, La Rochefoucauld alludes to the sea and to the life force as metaphors of his outlook. Both images occur in the *Réflexions diverses*, and although that work is not at the center of this study, it does highlight the maxim-writer's views. "De l'amour et de la mer" is short and may therefore be quoted in its entirety:

> Ceux qui ont voulu nous représenter l'amour et ses caprices l'ont comparé en tant de sortes à la mer qu'il est malaisé de rien ajouter à ce qu'ils en ont dit. Il nous ont fait voir que l'un et l'autre ont une inconstance et une infidélité égales, que leurs biens et leurs maux sont sans nombre, que les navigations les plus heureuses sont exposées à mille dangers, que les tempêtes et les écueils sont toujours à craindre, et que souvent même on fait naufrage dans le port. Mais en nous exprimant tant d'espérances et tant de craintes, ils ne nous ont pas assez montré, ce me semble, le rapport qu'il y a d'un amour usé, languissant et sur sa fin, à ces longues bonaces, à ces calmes ennuyeux, que l'on rencontre sous la ligne: on est fatigué d'un grand voyage, on souhaite de l'achever; on voit la terre, mais on manque de vent pour y arriver; on se voit exposé aux injures des saisons; les maladies et les langueurs empêchent d'agir; l'eau et les vivres manquent ou changent de goût; on a recours inutilement aux secours étrangers; on essaye de pêcher, et on prend quelques poissons, sans en tirer de soulagement ni de nourriture; on est las de tout ce qu'on voit, on est toujours avec ses mêmes pensées, et on est toujours ennuyé; on vit encore, et on a regret à vivre; on attend des désirs pour sortir d'un état pénible et languissant, mais on n'en forme que de faibles et d'inutiles. (Pp. 197-97)

This reflection contains many of La Rochefoucauld's ideas on love. In the first part he describes the internal chaos of love, its storms and reefs, and the second half is more concerned with the cycle of love, particularly with its end. Comparing love to the life rhythm in another of the *Réflexions diverses*, "De l'amour et de la vie," he picks up again the theme of cycle, of rhythm:

L'amour est une image de notre vie: l'un et l'autre sont sujets aux mêmes révolutions et aux mêmes changements. Leur jeunesse est pleine de joie et d'espérance: on se trouve heureux d'être jeune, comme on se trouve heureux d'aimer.
. . .
   Cette félicité néanmoins est rarement de longue durée, et elle ne peut conserver longtemps la grâce de la nouveauté. . . . Nous nous accoutumons à tout ce qui est à nous; les mêmes biens ne conservent pas leur même prix, . . . Cette inconstance involontaire est un effet du temps, qui prend malgré nous sur l'amour comme sur notre vie; il en efface insensiblement chaque jour un certain air de jeunesse et de gaieté, et en détruit les plus véritables charmes. (Pp. 200-201)

In these passages La Rochefoucauld demonstrates a decided proclivity for all that is associated with movement, time, and change. The *Maximes* also are filled with allusions to passage and to transformation. Love is conceived as a force totally dependent upon constant energy. Varying his elements, La Rochefoucauld adopts the metaphor of fire: "L'amour aussi bien que le feu ne peut subsister sans un mouvement continuel; et il cesse de vivre dès qu'il cesse d'espérer ou de craindre" (*Max.* 75). Not only, then, is love in a state of constant change and movement, rushing to an unfulfilling end, but it is conceived also as a projection, a forward-seeking shove, dependent upon either fear or hope, both future-directed emotions. La Rochefoucauld is thereby calling into question the very nature of love, perhaps its existence even; for if the dynamic element, the projection, is removed, there remains nothing. Love emerges as a non-force, dependent for sustenance upon our desires and anxieties, and it is these forces that sweep over us, demanding satisfaction.[16] La Rochefoucauld, as seen in the *Réflexions diverses*, is equally aware of love as a cycle, hence the comparison to the life flow; and although there are a few images of the early stages of love—"La grâce de la nouveauté est à l'amour ce que la fleur est sur les fruits; elle y donne un lustre qui s'efface aisément, et qui ne revient jamais"

[45]

(*Max.* 274)—most of the adages are concerned with the end of love, with its eventual erosion and subsequent staleness. In the terminal stages, no pleasure remains, and the frequent reference to illness suggests a feeling of corporal decrepitude, of a worn-out, worn-down mass of tissue. Stagnation sets in, and all that is left is a hopeless feeling of shame: "Il n'y a guère de gens qui ne soient honteux de s'être aimés quand ils ne s'aiment plus" (*Max.* 71). But worse than anything else is the inability to remove oneself from the labyrinth, from the web: "On a bien de la peine à rompre, quand on ne s'aime plus" (*Max.* 351), and the individual stagnates in the morass of his own dilemma.

The image of stagnated, dying love pervades both the *Maximes* and the *Réflexions diverses*, and once in a while, La Rochefoucauld makes allusion to the graceful, happy stages of a developing passion. There are, however, almost no references to love as a potent, positive force. That love may be a powerfully upsetting feeling, with negative effects, La Rochefoucauld does acknowledge: "Si on juge de l'amour par la plupart de ses effets, il ressemble plus à la haine qu'à l'amitié" (*Max.* 72). But most frequently, it is associated with weakness, debilitation, sickness, and death; once in a while with delicate, promising hopes; almost never with vitality and vigor. There is one important exception, however, indicating that La Rochefoucauld at the very least did glimpse the possibilities of something more powerful, more forceful: "La même fermeté qui sert à résister à l'amour sert aussi à le rendre violent et durable, et les personnes faibles qui sont toujours agitées des passions n'en sont presque jamais véritablement remplies" (*Max.* 477). Here love is linked to notions of energy and force; it is stationary ("durable") but not stagnant. Nevertheless, it seems fair to conclude that such possibilities are limited in La Rochefoucauld's moral universe—the note of disintegration prevails.

The final question revolves around *le vrai amour*, a concept that La Rochefoucauld developed at length in *La Justification de l'amour*, and that also occupies an important place in the *Maximes*. Nevertheless, the latter work fails to establish a working plan for this superior ethic, whereas the *Justification*, in an elaborate display of *mondanité*, offers the *honnête homme* a code for achieving harmonious interaction between his personal and social needs. The concept of true love in the *Maximes* is no longer a perfectioning of the Epicurean mode, combined with the excellence of *mondain* principles; it is instead an intangible, even quixotic, vision, an ideal value, that La Rochefoucauld periodically injects into his writing as a tantalizing standard. Moreover, it is truly indefinable, and the sole method of explanation is through defining what it is not.

Several maxims allude to the difficulty of defining this ideal, and almost all of these center upon the basic theme of concealment:

> S'il y a un amour pur et exempt du mélange de nos autres passions, c'est celui qui est caché au fond du coeur, et que nous ignorons nous-mêmes. (*Max.* 69)

> Il n'y a que d'une sorte d'amour, mais il y en a mille différentes copies. (*Max.* 74)

> Il est du véritable amour comme de l'apparition des esprits: tout le monde en parle, mais peu de gens en ont vu. (*Max.* 76)

The allusions to the hidden depths of the heart, if interpreted within the context of all of La Rochefoucauld's writings, would point to his doubt regarding the possibility of ever reaching such a pure form of love, for *le fond du coeur* is really a never ending abyss, and man can never hope to come to grips with its depths. Similarly, maxim 76, by comparing "real love" to apparitions, thereby contests its reality for mankind and places the whole question in the realm of the superstitious. In the aphorisms that which is secret and hidden is no longer the conscious effort of *l'honnête homme* to maintain the restraints of his moral system. Rather, if *le vrai amour* is hidden, it is because the ideal is far removed from any hope of realization.

And yet the ideal remains strong, appears almost viable sometimes, but ultimately remains elusive. Of course, were one to achieve such purity, all coquetry, gallantry, envy, and jealousy would disappear. But the final reality is an imperfect state of love, an inauthentic copy.

Evidently, as Jean Starobinski has concluded, La Rochefoucauld never succumbed to the Nietzschean type of nihilism he flirted with; for he maintained at least a facade of belief in absolute moral values, unattainable perhaps, but existing as images in man's mind.[17] Certain religious, ethical, and moral standards—in this case, love— retain their sense of purity, if only in the abstract. There is still a metaphysical and psychological "out," and fundamental, humanistic notions—freedom, will, self-perfection— are given a new lift, after having been negated.

It is, however, difficult to return to the *Justification* after the *Maximes*; for even if the latter fail to take the ultimate step into a form of nihilism, they offer nonetheless some rather conclusive statements on the "way things are," statements that seem to destroy the hope that was put forth in the apology on love. There is an element of finality to the maxims, whereas the apology of love proposes an "open end," an aperture onto the world.

1.  Jean Starobinski, "La Rochefoucauld et les morales substitutives," *Nouvelle Revue française* 14 (July 1966): 16-34; (August 1966): 211-29.

2.  Roland Barthes, "Littérature et discontinu," in *Essais critiques* (Paris: Editions du Seuil, 1964), p. 178.

3.  La Rochefoucauld, *La Justification de l'amour*, ed. J. D. Hubert (Paris: A. G. Nizet, 1971). Subsequent references are to this edition, and will be found in the text.

4.  Jean Starobinski, "Complexité de La Rochefoucauld," *Preuves*, No. 135 (May 1962), pp. 35-36.

5.  La Rochefoucauld, *Maximes*, ed. Jacques Truchet (Paris: Garnier Frères, 1967), p. 10. Subsequently, the maxim number will be cited in the text. (References are to the 1678 edition of the *Maximes* unless otherwise noted.) The same method will be used for quotations from the *Réflexions diverses*, which have been published in the same edition (Garnier) as the *Maximes*; the page number, however, will be given.

Other passages in La Rochefoucauld's works support the theory of multiple motivation, notably the head maxim of the 1678 edition: "Ce que nous prenons pour des vertus n'est souvent qu'un assemblage de diverses actions et de divers intérêts, que la fortune ou notre industrie savent arranger; et ce n'est pas toujours par valeur et par chasteté que les hommes sont vaillants, et que les femmes sont chastes." A section from the long maxim on *l'amour-propre*, which was expunged after the first edition, states that it is "inconstant d'inconstance, de légèreté, d'amour, de nouveauté, de lassitude et de dégoût."

6. Starobinski, "La Rochefoucauld et les morales substitutives," pp. 16-17.

7. Hubert admits to this possibility in his introduction.

8. Perhaps seeking to modify his position on the topic, La Rochefoucauld removed several important maxims in the later editions. In the Truchet edition they are grouped together as *maximes supprimées*, following a long tradition of La Rochefoucauld's editors.

9. Starobinski, "La Rochefoucauld et les morales substitutives," p. 16.

10. Philip Lewis, "La Rochefoucauld: The Rationality of Play," *Yale French Studies*, no. 41 (1964), p. 144.

11. Ibid.

12. May Wendeline Butrick, "The Concept of Love in the *Maxims* of La Rochefoucauld," (Ph.D. diss., State University of Iowa, 1959), p. 87.

13. Lewis, "La Rochefoucauld," p. 145.

14. I am following the order established by Jacques Truchet in his edition of the *Maximes*, that is, by the date of their removal after the first edition.

15. Starobinski, "La Rochefoucauld et les morales substitutives," p. 16.

16. This is not the first time that La Rochefoucauld questions the existence of a separate, independent force called "love." Maxim 68 proceeds in a similar fashion: "Il est difficile de définir l'amour. Ce qu'on en peut dire est que dans l'âme c'est une passion de régner, dans les esprits c'est une sympathie, et dans le corps ce n'est qu'une envie cachée et délicate de posséder ce que l'on aime après beaucoup de mystères." The "ce qu'on en peut dire" successfully challenges any certainty of what love is and replaces precision ("définir") with vagueness. It is not, subsequently, only the language that is vague, but perhaps our entire concept of love. In any case, according to the maxim, all three of the components are at once love and not love, but each has a separate, independent name and, hence, existence.

17. Starobinski, "La Rochefoucauld et les morales substitutives," pp. 25-26.

Chapter Three

# MADAME DE LAFAYETTE

ENDANT QUE LA GUERRE CIVILE déchirait la France sous le règne de Charles IX, l'Amour ne laissait pas de trouver sa place parmi tant de désordres et d'en causer beaucoup plus dans son Empire."[1] The abrupt beginning of *La Princesse de Montpensier* and its direct thrust upon the reader succeed in translating perfectly the view of passion as a violent, interrupting force in a world dependent upon monotonous repetition, upon unquestioned habit, for smooth functioning. In Mme de Lafayette's works, true passion results from a sudden shock, from the arrival on the scene of a new presence, unknown before, and capable of radically altering the existence of the participants. It is not by chance that the opening lines of *La Princesse de Montpensier* establish a link between love and war. The martial metaphor for Mme de Lafayette, as for La Rochefoucauld, was the most potent means of expressing the state of man subject to invasion by violent passions that call into question his yearnings toward repose as well as his belief in free will.

It is the explosive, destructive, anarchical force of Eros that Mme de Lafayette sought to depict. Under the decency of style (or the style of decency), the mind and the body are warring, the former manifestly unable to exert control over the spontaneous, free impulses of the latter. In the tradition of the Rambouillet group and of the *précieux* code in general, passionate love could be traced to an origin of mutual understanding and admiration.[2] In other words, it has a past. But for Mme de Lafayette, passion originates explosively, combustively, and is not related at all to the mental concepts of esteem and respect, based upon prior knowledge.

Originating spontaneously within the body, erotic passion is translated by the body, totally unreceptive to the dicta of virtue and common sense. This *coup de foudre* effect occurs on successive occasions in *La Princesse de Clèves*: M. de Clèves, upon seeing Mlle de Chartres for the first time, "demeura si touché de sa beauté et de l'air modeste qu'il avait remarqué dans ses actions qu'on peut dire qu'il conçut pour elle dès ce moment une passion et une estime extraordinaires."[3] When Mme de Clèves and the duc de Nemours first meet at a court ball, the effect is absolutely electric and does not fail to astonish all who surround them: "Quand ils commencèrent à danser, il s'éleva dans la salle un murmure de louanges. Le roi et les reines se souvinrent qu'ils ne s'étaient jamais vus, et trouvèrent quelque chose de singulier de les voir danser ensemble sans se connaître" (p. 262). The moment a new passion is born, it is sufficient unto itself, and, originating in the demands of the body, is totally free from dependency upon the past.

That the body's impulses offer the most direct truth concerning the individual is perceived, although unconsciously, by the king and queens. Vaguely troubled, they react to this scene of perfect physical harmony by seeking to reinstall through a rapid introduction the reign of reason and virtue signaled by the term "se connaître." The instant, spontaneous accord between Mme de Clèves and the duc de Nemours is in violation of traditional codes—occidental, humanist, *précieux*—seeking to spiritualize love.

The entire story of Zaïde (in the tale of that name) and Consalve also belies the *précieux*, devout humanist conception of love based upon prior knowledge, admiration, and

[52]

respect. Early in the tale, Consalve expresses the belief that he could never love a woman without first knowing her well; the prince, his friend, takes the opposite stance (the whole discussion recalling a long tradition in *courtois* literature, the debate on love, from the medieval *jeux partis* to the *précieux* novel): "Je serais incapable de devenir amoureux d'une personne avec qui je serais accoutumé et, si je ne suis surpris d'abord, je ne puis être touché. Je crois que les inclinations naturelles se font sentir dans les premiers moments; et les passions, qui ne viennent que par le temps, ne se peuvent appeler de véritables passions."[4] Consalve falls passionately in love with Zaïde from the first moment he lays eyes on her and thus contradicts his own theory of prior acquaintance.[5] The obvious conclusion from Consalve's experience is that the nature of passion is sudden, violent, interruptive, independent of control by reason or by will.

Because Mme de Lafayette clothed her tales and novels in a habit of cold concision, where the voice of passion central to her writing adopts only the most lucid, structured, carefully modulated tones, the very obvious erotic center of the works is frequently shunned in criticism, as if to penetrate the style would be a transgression. Although criticism has not failed to point out that one of the major themes of the novels and *nouvelles* is the difficult transition between appearance and reality—hence the lengthy portrayal of courtly splendor in the early pages of *La Princesse de Clèves*, contrasting with the moral imperfection that soon follows—it has, nonetheless, not carried such analysis one step further by showing that Mme de Lafayette's careful masking (through the channels of monotonous repetition, barren vocabulary, rigid structure) was only that, a mask, an appearance that barely veiled the erotic center and the diverse inner tensions.[6]

It is true that allusions to the violent demands of the body, to the preeminence of the erotic over the mind and its illusions of will, may be stylistically reduced in Mme de Lafayette's works. The sole exception to this general pat-

[53]

tern of minimal portrayal of that which is directly, explicitly sexual is the short, posthumous *La Comtesse de Tende* where the "language" of the body belies the code of decency, social and literary. Sensual fulfillment is ushered in, expressed obviously through recourse to adultery, pregnancy, and illegitimate birth. The guilty participants are punished severely, but for a short time, the duration only of the tale itself (the illusion of fiction translating the illusory situation of a reigning, satisfied desire), the code of erotic gratification presides. The language of the text is virtually "violated" by the intrusion of vocabulary such as *grossesse*, but with the death of the heroine, the temporary social and literary deviation is expunged.

Contemporary writers have the option of adopting the most primitive discourse in attempting to translate the outcry of passion. Neither grammar nor stylistic euphemism is required. Language can be not only direct but obscene in its effort to capture spontaneity, intensity, and violence. These same emotions were hardly absent from the literature of the classical age, but they were reduced or modulated by an extraordinary superstructure. The chaos of passion was thematically present, but linguistically ordered. Phèdre's lamentations, for example, over the tremendous burden and pain of her body, are cloaked in the rigid, highly structured Alexandrine verse:

> Que ces vains ornements, que ces voiles me pèsent!
> Quelle importune main, en formant tous ces noeuds,
> A pris soin sur mon front d'assembler mes cheveux?
> Tout m'afflige, et me nuit, et conspire à me nuire.[7]

The body's disorder and pain are couched in poetry's contained refinement, the structure of the verse lending structure to, and thereby instantly diminishing, the effect of emotional chaos. In a similar fashion, mythological symbolism replaces more direct allusions while offering unambiguous explanation. That Hippolyte is painted as "ce fils de l'Amazone" serves notice that there will be a struggle with the opposite sex.

[54]

For Mme de Lafayette the relaxation of the socio-literary code occurs directly only in *La Comtesse de Tende*. Her other works are free of obvious violations. Hence, the recourse is to sexual symbolism as in the second scene at Coulommiers in *La Princesse de Clèves*, a scene that Michel Butor has analyzed thoroughly. Butor suggests that such symbolism, in this case, *la canne des Indes*, perceived by us in the post-Freudian age, was also discernible to the seventeenth-century reader accustomed to its frequent use in the fairy tales of the age.[8] (I will discuss later Mme de Lafayette's recourse to various elements derived from the *romanesque* and the atmosphere of the *contes de fée*.)

Although the truth of their extraordinary mutual attraction is already sensed by Mme de Clèves and M. de Nemours, it remains at first an unconscious, hidden perception. Within the boundaries of a socially acceptable act—dancing—an act that is moreover ordered by social authority (it is the king who commands them to dance), the power of the body's extremely forceful presence and vitality is at once lessened and harmonized. The experience is still perceived as basically aesthetically satisfying; the beauty of the couple provokes "un murmure de louanges," although, imperceptibly, there is already the beginning of a transgression, for the couple has never met before. But the physical harmony takes precedence over any sense of imminent danger, and the sexual nature of the pleasure the two partners experience is hidden by the veil of social acceptability and by the structured, measured elegance of the dance.

At Coulommiers, however, a different mood prevails; and although Mme de Clèves lives the entire scene in a blur of conscious and subconscious, of dream and reality, the moment posits the entirety of her conflict. What was before socially authorized becomes now a transgression, an intrusion, a penetration that threatens to destroy not only Mme de Clèves but the entire social network based upon a norm of control and restraint.

There is, in particular, at Coulommiers, a sense of underlying violence that menaces directly the person of Mme de Clèves. Her utter exposure to Nemours, the penetration of his look upon her, testify to strong male aggression. The game of love, as Bernard Pingaud has shown, is not played without some extreme consequences for the woman: "Un homme peut bien conquérir et abandonner successivement plusieurs maîtresses. Une femme, surtout si elle est mariée, perd à ce jeu non seulement la considération, mais le repos. Cette aventure qui n'est pour les autres qu'un sujet de curiosité, auquel on s'attache un jour et qu'on oublie le lendemain, est pour elle une déchéance progressive, contre laquelle, par tous les moyens en son pouvoir, elle essaie en vain de lutter."[9] Throughout all of Mme de Lafayette's works—in her fiction as well as in the short biography of Henriette d'Angleterre—there is a pervading atmosphere of male prowess that exerts itself either in the game of war or in the game of love. No less than four men attempt to control the princesse de Montpensier, each regarding her as his own exclusive conquest. The comte de Tende freely neglects his wife, subjects her to pain and humiliation, until his passion is eventually ignited through jealousy. And the duc de Nemours persistently views the relationship with Mme de Clèves in terms of an aggressive seduction.

Women are the prey of virile, violent instincts, and martial activity is seen by Mme de Lafayette as the sole satisfactory means to repressing aggressive, erotic impulses. Thus when the chevalier de Guise fully comprehends Mme de Clèves' feelings for Nemours, he is so grieved that "dès ce jour, il prit la résolution de ne penser jamais à être aimé de Mme de Clèves. Mais pour quitter cette entreprise, qui lui avait paru si difficile et si glorieuse, il en fallait quelque autre dont la grandeur pût l'occuper. Il se mit dans l'esprit de prendre Rhodes, dont il avait déjà eu quelque pensée" (p. 307). Aggressive energies must be released in some fashion, and war is perhaps the sole satisfactory outlet in a world where passion is rarely capable of being gratified and, when it is, of enduring. Women are perceived as the object of the male impulse to vanquish, and the acts of transgression that their lovers commit leave them in a highly weakened position.

In *La Comtesse de Tende*, the most direct attack is of course the adultery that triumphs over female virtue, exposing the countess to guilt and dishonor. But although the reader is never witness to any adulterous scene (we are told only that she has become pregnant), a strong preliminary violation occurs when the chevalier de Navarre successfully enters her chambers, surreptitiously, thus penetrating beyond the limits of socially acceptable meeting grounds. This violation is, moreover, keenly felt as such by the countess; she perceives a direct threat to her person and reputation. The entering of a room is in itself, for Mme de Lafayette, an act of seduction over a weakened adversary, who quickly succumbs to irresolution and confusion: "La comtesse se laissa tomber sur un lit de repos, dont elle s'était relevée à demi et, regardant le chevalier avec des yeux pleins d'amour et de larmes: Vous voulez donc que je meure? lui dit-elle. Croyez-vous qu'un coeur puisse contenir tout ce que vous me faites sentir?"[10] The chevalier's triumph, his successful attempt at drawing out the confession of love, is flawless.

It is, however, in *La Princesse de Clèves* that Mme de Lafayette constructs her most masterful scene of symbolic rape. Early in the chain of events, Nemours freely steals a portrait of Mme de Clèves, and the symbolic possession is reinforced by his knowledge that the portrait belongs to M. de Clèves. The princess observes the entire scene, not at first without considerable pleasure. However, the ravishment is soon perceived as an aggressive attack on her person: "Elle fit réflexion à la violence de l'inclination qui l'entraînait vers M. de Nemours; elle trouva qu'elle n'était plus maîtresse de ses paroles et de son visage" (p. 303). For the moment Mme de Clèves has been successfully undermined.

The desired goal is physical possession, and this triumph of Eros is shared completely by the woman, although she is never the aggressor. She may flee, as does the princesse de Clèves, succumb as the comtesse de Tende, but she is not the initiator of the struggle to possess. If she does choose to withstand the attack, her conscious behavior may well conform to her prescribed rules; but her subconscious, through her body, her gestures, her almost imperceptible movements and reactions, succeeds in communicating her yearnings. The body announces exactly what the mind seeks to obliterate. The mark of erotic passion is the complete inability to disguise it, and the spontaneous expression of this passion—unnatural silences, blushes, self-conscious gestures[11]—is the surest sign of the mind's loss of control. Originating in the body, erotic love is translated totally by it; and the upsetting, disquieting effect of passion upon the individual cannot be successfully masked. The dancing scene in *La Princesse de Clèves* reveals itself as the moment of optimum candor; here the basic truth of spontaneous drives is neither blocked outwardly nor repressed inwardly.

The nature of passion, as portrayed in Mme de Lafayette's universe, is to ravage, to destroy the smooth continuum of existence, to alienate the self from its most intimate conception. Surging suddenly, seemingly from nowhere, endowed with no past, no socially sanctioned signs (knowledge, respect), passionate love is experienced as a radical break, both temporal and psychological. In *La Princesse de Clèves*, which is the most complete of all Mme de Lafayette's works (the other tales offer more or less diverse fragments of the whole cycle), the goal is to reestablish the integrity of the heroine. Mme de Chartres' recourse to a vocabulary of imminent danger, of fall—"vous êtes sur le bord du précipice (pp. 277)—suggests that at stake is the concept of "breaking apart," of falling from one world into another, engendering dispersion of the self and its alienation from a preliminary set of values.

The problem then becomes, once the disquieting force of passion sets in, how to recompose the self, how to reestablish continuity, how to regain the lost sense of "oneness." The battle was hardly a new one in the century, and Mme de Lafayette's writings seem to bear directly upon the solutions of her predecessors, if only to deny their ideas. The whole of *La Princesse de Clèves*, from one point of view, is designed to combat a perspective of life based upon the strength of the mind. With the example of Consalve, M. de Clèves, and the princesse de Clèves herself, Mme de Lafayette quickly and forcefully undermines Mlle de Scudéry's and the *précieuses'* belief in mutual understanding and admiration as a prerequisite to a satisfactory love relationship. The body, and not the mind, is the seat of passion, and therefore any struggle to resist it based upon reason and lucid discourse is doomed to failure.

Descartes, whose *Les Passions de l'âme* is perhaps at the base of Mme de Lafayette's thought, wrote that it was possible to acquire "un empire très absolu sur toutes les passions, si on employait assez d'industrie à les dresser et à les conduire,"[12] through the practice of *la vertu* (a predominating word, moreover, of *La Princesse de Clèves* and certainly not by chance the final one). *La vertu* was considered as the exercise of those standards that an *honnête homme* would judge to be superior. The necessary factor ensuring the continuity of this standard was "une ferme et constante résolution d'en bien user, c'est-à-dire de ne manquer jamais de volonté pour entreprendre et exécuter toutes les choses qu'il jugera être les meilleures."[13] The concept of a resolution relies heavily upon the firm use of mental faculties to moderate the force of the passions and endows the "word" with ultimate powers of transcendence.

This path is foredoomed a failure by Mme de Lafayette, however, for, as Serge Doubrovsky has expressed, "la réflexion, comme son nom l'indique, ne fait que refléter les pensées que nous avons formées spontanément et sur lesquelles elle n'a aucune prise."[14] Mme de Clèves' multifold attempts at extricating herself from her prison miscarry because they are based upon language that is manifestly unable to reply to the body's spontaneous drives.

Mme de Chartres, in an effort to regulate her daughter's behavior on the side of virtue, depended upon a system of self-control, obtained in turn by a constantly on-going dialogue with the self in favor of certain moral values, the antipode of which is the disorganizing life of passion. This "extrême défiance de soi-même" (p. 248) is reached only via an unremitting inner soliloquy; the "right" words will achieve the desired goal of virtue. Thus the resolutions that Mme de Clèves makes after each emotional jolt are her chosen method of breaking the cycle.

After her portrait is stolen, after she reads the letter supposedly addressed to Nemours (the one that in reality was directed to the vidame de Chartres), after she spends time alone with Nemours in an effort to copy that letter from memory, Mme de Clèves, aware of her violently intense feelings for him, resolves to control herself, to re-establish reason in her life, to combat her passion. But this task will prove impossible, although she fully believes that her resolutions in themselves are sufficient to do battle with her desires.

In the moments following her reading of the letter, Mme de Clèves, totally absorbed in her remorse and guilt, is consoled by the recognition that, "après cette connaissance, elle n'avait plus rien à craindre d'elle-même, et qu'elle serait entièrement guérie de l'inclination qu'elle avait pour ce prince" (p. 311). Later, however, after the moments of solitude with Nemours in an effort to reconstruct the letter, moments that bring her considerable pleasure, she concludes: "Je suis vaincue et surmontée par une inclination qui m'entraîne malgré moi. Toutes mes résolutions sont inutiles; je pensai hier tout ce que je pense aujourd'hui et je fais aujourd'hui tout le contraire de ce que je résolus hier" (p. 330). With the full recognition of the impotence of the private, inner word, of reflections, in controlling her emotional state, Mme de Clèves opts for the sole remaining solution, flight: "Il faut m'arracher de la présence de M. de Nemours; il faut m'en aller à la campagne, quelque bizarre que puisse paraître mon voyage" (p.

330). But flight in this universe is tightly constricted, and
M. de Nemours has only to visit his sister, whose country
home is a neighbor to Coulommiers, in order to be present
at the scene of the *aveu*.

Flight is not an answer to the dilemma, for the locus is
at once too restrained, and the heroine is constantly being
called back to the even more intimate circle of the court.
Feeling these parallel pressures upon her, Mme de Clèves
returns to reliance upon the lucid, unequivocal word as a
solution to her problem, only this time she chooses discourse not with herself but with her husband. The question
of a sincere confession is not a new one in the history of
*La Princesse de Clèves*. Mme de Chartres had maintained
a strict relationship with her daughter, whereby the latter
was to keep her mother informed of all the amorous in-
trigues developing about this newcomer to the court, a
counsel the heroine follows until the encounter with Nemours. After the episode at the ball, Mme de Clèves enters
into a whole new world, that of the secret. And when she
finally resolves to speak openly to her mother, it is too late;
Mme de Chartres is on her deathbed, unable to communicate at length. In the early pages of the work, the power of
the word is still at its highest peak. Mme de Chartres relies
upon it as the sole method of maintaining her daughter in
a virtuous state. Nonetheless, when Mme de Clèves perceives the nature of her feelings, she abruptly falls silent,
and communication is cut off or disguised.

The *aveu*, the confession to her husband is doomed, for
it opposes two codes, two universes, that are radically
unharmonious: the mind and the body, Logos and Eros. It
has been questioned whether the *aveu* is truly an act of
courage on the part of Mme de Clèves or, rather, its
opposite, a wish to place the responsibility for her conduct
on someone else. Possibly it is both. What is more significant, however, is whether, as an act relying upon the power
of reasoned discourse, it can successfully combat passion
and jealousy. It seems fair to judge it a failure, for the
prince de Clèves, although intellectually esteeming his

[61]

wife's sincerity, is manifestly unable to control his rage for possession. Her "Fiez-vous à mes paroles" becomes an impossibility; M. de Clèves' suspicions will arise not out of logic, not out of dispassionate reason, but out of his frustrated effort to appropriate Mme de Clèves for himself. Belief, trust, and confidence are of perilously little weight in a world where the humanistic code has been stripped bare. What is sought is complete possession over *l'autre*— Eros being the symbol for that possession as well as for its eventual failure—and words are impotent as agents against this rage.

In the end it appears that there are really only two alternatives: to succumb, as do Mme de Tende and the princesse de Montpensier, or to fight, in accordance with the *honnête* code: resolutions, sincerity, and flight. The second choice, which may loosely be referred to as an attempt to repress, is unsatisfactory, for the spontaneous drives of the body will not be controlled by the dicta of the conscience grounded into the format of *la parole*. The transcendence of the passions that occurs in Corneille's plays reveals itself as totally bankrupt in Mme de Lafayette's moral structure, and the desire for possession, translated through the concept of sexual desire and energies, emerges as the superior force. Descartes' code of *générosité*, his heavy use of *la réflexion* is shown to be equally lacking, since the inner dialogue, the reasoning with the self, comes too late. The spontaneous drives of the body have preempted the reign of the mind.

If attempts at repressing fail, as they inevitably do, then the obvious alternative would be that of the two other heroines: to give in. La comtesse de Tende experiences the totality of her decision; la princesse de Montpensier succumbs in intentions only. Both women are severely "punished," through great suffering and eventual death; and within the context of these two tales, it would appear that a strict Christian moral alone prevents a happy conclusion. There is a strong sense of transgression, of having given in to the body, which a rigid Christian ethic cannot tolerate. This ethic unquestionably permeates the writings of Mme de Lafayette. The erotic is seen as threatening and demeaning; women are prey to the seductive efforts of the male; transgressions occur that violate the most traditional, religious views. But the full cycle of Mme de Lafayette's thinking is really not complete in either *La Princesse de Montpensier* or *La Comtesse de Tende*, for in these two tales physical desire is merely punished. It is not shown as an empty path to possession as in the far more complex *La Princesse de Clèves*. The drive to appropriate *l'autre*, interpreted through erotic longing, emerges as a radical impossibility, and it is to this end that Mme de Lafayette's works are directed. Physical possession is recognized as vastly unable to satisfy the far more intense longing for control.

The theme runs strongly through *La Princesse de Clèves*, interwoven among others, almost lost at times, but looming up at the end, thereby giving new force to what was earlier not quite conclusive. The failure of Eros to satisfy on any level beyond immediate gratification is evident early in the marriage between M. de Clèves and Mlle de Chartres, prior even to her first encounter with Nemours:

> M. de Clèves ne trouva pas que Mlle de Chartres eût changé de sentiment en changeant de nom. La qualité de mari lui donna de plus grands privilèges; mais elle ne lui donna pas une autre place dans le coeur de sa femme. Cela fit aussi que, pour être son mari, il ne laissa pas d'être son amant, parce qu'il avait toujours quelque chose à souhaiter au delà de sa possession; et, quoiqu'elle vécut parfaitement bien avec lui, il n'était pas entièrement heureux. Il conservait pour elle une passion violente et inquiète qui troublait sa joie. (P. 260)

The vague, nebulous quality that surrounds this passage, the imprecision of the "quelque chose," is not by accident. Rather, Mme de Lafayette's efforts here seem directed to portraying a still subconscious perception, experienced fully by M. de Clèves but not in a lucid, comprehensive fashion, only within the realm of dim impressions. Having attained full rights and "privilèges" over his wife, whom he adored and desired from their first encounter, having "possessed" her physically, he remains unsatisfied. Although aware from the start that Mlle de Chartres never shared his passion, he undoubtedly anticipated that physical intimacy, achieved in marriage, would establish the intensity he had sought.

The queen, in her pursuit of the vidame de Chartres, expresses directly, almost violently, what was lolling about in M. de Clèves' mind. She offers the most brutal recognition of man's desires, seeking to appropriate the vidame de Chartres exclusively for herself, forever, and she will entertain no other attachments for him:

> Je le souhaite, parce que je désire que vous soyez entière-
> ment attaché à moi, et qu'il serait impossible que je fusse
> contente de votre amitié si vous étiez amoureux. . . .
> Souvenez-vous que je veux la vôtre [confiance] tout entière;
> que je veux que vous n'ayez ni ami, ni amie, que ceux qui
> me seront agréables, et que vous abandonniez tout autre
> soin que celui de me plaire. (P. 317)

This absolute attachment, this fidelity with no end, is impossible to achieve, for it is truly a confiscation of *l'autre*, a denial of his autonomy.

But conscious desire to possess is rare in Mme de Lafayette's tales; more frequently, the wish plays itself out at the subconscious level. The ultimate failure to appropriate the partner is subconsciously perceived by certain characters long before emotional involvement has become a reality. It has been noted that Mme de Lafayette's works most frequently center upon a trio,[15] the third person serving as the obstacle to the satisfaction of the two others. The trio structure is quite naturally a symbol in itself of the inability of the couple to re-create the "edenic isolation,"[16] and a symbol also of the jealousy inherent in all passion. But the banal character of the trio structure is invested with an additional force when the metaphor of

[64]

"threeness" becomes a subliminal response and an obstacle to the mere project of the couple.

M. de Clèves falls victim to these strange, unconscious machinations, for his illness and his subsequent death result, not from any real situation, but from his fantasy of Mme de Clèves spending the night with Nemours. Without waiting to hear any precise details from his aide, who had observed Nemours at Coulommiers (for indeed, those precise details were lacking, since nothing occurred), he succumbs to a violent illness immediately, almost as if he could no longer endure the pain of not having achieved with his wife the relationship he had so ardently desired. His imagination, evoking fantasies based on the structure of a trio, becomes his sole defense against any further hopes for attaching Mme de Clèves exclusively to his own person. Illness and death are thus his only way out of the unsatisfactory "coupling" with his wife. Imagination becomes the means to freedom, to M. de Clèves' liberation from illusions of "quelque chose . . . au-delà de sa possession," of an existence devoted exclusively to himself.

The novel *Zaïde* is too reminiscent of the earlier trends of the *romanesque*, too different from the *nouveau roman* of Mme de Lafayette, to enter easily into an analysis. The structure of the work hardly conforms with the new trend toward brevity and concision. But certain themes in the set of tales do reappear in all of Mme de Lafayette's writings. The hero, Consalve, involved in a passionate effort to woo Zaïde, very early in the novel constructs for himself an elaborate rationalization of her emotional distance. Not able to understand her language, he still perceives through various gestures and reactions that she is in love with another, and the intensity with which he endows this fiction points. to a fundamental sense of frustration inherent in many of Mme de Lafayette's principal characters. His imaginary construct serves as a solid barrier to all his hopes, as if in advance, on the subliminal level alone, the perception of the ultimate failure of all coupling is already present.

With Consalve the story takes another turn and ends with

references to a happy marriage. But his addiction to anxieties over the threat of a rival, a nonexistent one, prefigures entirely the situation of Alphonse and Bélasire, whose short tale seems to serve no further end than to demonstrate in precise terms the subconscious blocking of fulfillment. Alphonse is presented as a man with a primary obsession, a fear of jealousy, that guides his life and allows him no serious attachment until he meets Bélasire. In the early part of his relationship with her, he remains tortured with doubts about marriage, preferring "le malheur de vivre sans Bélasire à celui de vivre avec elle sans être aimé" (p. 110). On a conscious level, he manages to surmount these fears; but the subconscious refuses to follow such a facile accommodation, and in a sudden, seemingly inexplicable transition, Alphonse passes from confidence to doubt, the lack of intervention on the part of the author testifying to the movement away from the conscious and toward the subliminal. Alphonse enmeshes himself in a paroxysm of jealousy for a rival, but he is a dead rival and can pose no threat to the harmony of the couple. As with Consalve, there is an extraordinary intensity to Alphonse's struggle that belies an almost deliberate attempt at destroying the relationship with Bélasire, as if his psyche, conditioned by a long tradition of suspicion toward marriage, fully anticipated the impossibility of having her exclusively for himself. Although his conscious mind at this time has gone beyond his fears and all his efforts are directed toward marriage, in reality his longstanding revolt emerges triumphant over his voluntary decisions. The transition from conscious confidence to subliminal rebellion is almost imperceptible; it is not analyzed or interpreted by Mme de Lafayette, for it is not a movement of reason but rather a complex, subconscious impulse. Thus the construct of the false trio serves Alphonse as a potent means to a radical rupture of the relationship.

It is not always through the device of a hypothetical trio that the perception of the ultimate inability to "possess" is manifested. Mme de Clèves eventually foresees how fragile is the duc de Nemours' attachment for her, how time alone will destroy it, how she can never, in fact, retain him. Hers is the recognition that passion can subsist only when barred from total satisfaction. Within the context of *La Princesse de Clèves*, the fading is seen occurring on the part of M. de Nemours, on the part of the male, and that may well have been Mme de Lafayette's bias; but it is precisely the same course that Alphonse long feared on the part of the woman. It is a pattern perceived as operating within the "other," but that is its psychological base. Metaphysically it is the recognition of the impossibility of possession.

The princesse de Clèves' problem, and Alphonse's problem as well, remain without obvious solution, for the paradox of the life situation will not allow for a compromise. "En face d'une double impossibilité métaphysique,—l'amour ne pouvant être satisfait, en raison des relations qui existent nécessairement entre deux libertés, ni refoulé, du fait qu'il représente une irrésistible expression de nous-mêmes,—il ne reste plus de solution, ou plutôt il n'en reste qu'une: *le suicide*. Si la spontanéité ne peut être réprimée, elle peut être supprimée, et la destruction de soi est la seule issue."[17] A self-mutilation occurs; for the princesse de Clèves it is a solitary sacrifice; for Alphonse and Bélasire, the couple unite in an effort to annihilate their potentiality as two. Alphonse's intense subconscious drive to destroy any hopes of marriage is in the end consented to, and surpassed by, Bélasire herself. Establishing the preeminence of *le repos*, Bélasire renounces all further commerce with Alphonse and, going one step further, commits herself to a life without love by entering a convent. The renunciation is virtually a mutual one, with the couple united in a stand against marriage, against love, against the foredoomed attempt at possession. In the interest of repose, of avoiding the tumultuous jealousy that is inseparable from passion (for it announces the failure to possess), the couple will be sacrificed, sacrifices itself, destroys itself voluntarily. Bélasire's retreat is thus a spiritual suicide, a denial of what is most fundamental, spontaneous, and free, a mutilation of her person and equally of Alphonse, for the couple-structure is ruptured.

Mme de Clèves, in an even more extreme stance, chooses not only a spiritual suicide but a physical one as well, as if recognizing that the only way out of the dilemma of unsatisfied passion is the death of the instrument that is the seat of the longing: the body. The illness that debilitates her and leads to her death becomes the means by which she successfully purges her passion. Death installs itself in the place of Eros, in a revival of the Tristan myth.

There is, as Gabriel Bounoure has remarked, a strong element of *auto-punition*[18] implied in the renunciation of Mme de Clèves and of Alphonse-Bélasire, a self-chastisement for having played the game poorly and lost, of having succumbed to a pattern of living totally opposed to earlier, stricter standards of *vertu* and *défiance*. The retreat to the convent may be viewed as an aspiration to purity, to a life beyond the disorder engendered by love, as a means to moral healing, or as the perfect *clôture* translating the suppression of Eros. All these motives intertwine, quite naturally, and all come back to a more general theme of refusal dictated by aspirations toward repose.

If *le repos* here is essentially the absence of passion and suffering, then Mme de Clèves and Bélasire are basically opting for a minimal existence, a life characterized by absence rather than plenitude. The theme of repose traverses the moralist writings of the century, originating perhaps in the religious literature (Pascal, Bossuet), but finding room also in the ataraxia of the Epicureans. The tranquillity to which Mme de Lafayette's characters aspire is a strange paradox, at once an emptiness and a fulfillment—ultimately, a fulfillment in an emotional vacuum.

But if suppression is indeed the accurate word for the path that Mme de Lafayette sees as the sole "out" in a world where passion, desired eternal, rests finite, it is also the right one for her efforts to deny the most traditional forms of *romanesque* expression. The attack is thus against

[68]

the double illusion of the myth of passion and of its expression, the *précieux* novel. Reading through Mme de Lafayette's works, one perceives two distinct movements that compose the structure of the *récit*. There is the flat, monotonous, monochromatic repetition of certain basic passages: Mme de Clèves' continued efforts to reestablish the continuity of her emotional life; Consalve's slow, steady progression toward Zaïde. Varied only slightly each time, these passages form the foundation of each tale. Less frequently there are flashes of something else, scenes that are throwbacks to the traditional *romanesque*, sometimes even *conte de fée*, atmosphere. It is as if these latter scenes are there as traps, for no sooner do they surge upon the page than they are destroyed for the illusion that they create.

The early, descriptive pages of *La Princesse de Clèves* are among the snares; the superlative kings and queens, princes and princesses, dukes and duchesses, are portrayed in all their courtly splendor, only to "fall" rapidly into the most untenable situations far removed from aristocratic appearances. The dancing scene, also, stands out as an "interrupter" of the monotony, a moment when the illusion of harmony is at its peak, the atmosphere of the ball lending a highly *romanesque* flavor to the moment. The château of Mme de Clèves at Coulommiers is in itself a fantastic lure, the ideal and familiar place for the satisfaction of passion, the fairy-tale response to the problem. But the scenes at Coulommiers emerge as the antithesis of the *romanesque* experience. What is woven there is not satisfaction but rather the powerful destruction of any such possibility, for it is these scenes that are the cause of M. de Clèves' jealousy, illness, and death. Rather than opening onto a field of unlimited charms, of romantic play, they definitively shut out the possibility, the illusion, of a marriage between the princesse de Clèves and M. de Nemours. The chateau becomes the locus of death, belying its traditional wonderland symbolism.

This opposition of structures—the monotonous, flat scenes

[69]

pitted against the momentarily dramatic ones—is little more than the myth confronting the reality. The illusion of passion will be destroyed as will its medium, the long, adventure-laden *précieux* novel. Henceforth the tale will be short; *romanesque*-type episodes will be included in order for the illusion to be more systematically destroyed. Considerably more polished in her artistic skills by the time she wrote *La Princesse de Clèves* and thus able to avoid direct references to her method, Mme de Lafayette offered in her earlier works almost a commentary of her aims. In *La Princesse de Montpensier*, the first of her tales, she signals her intentions exactly and explicitly:

> Un jour qu'il revenait à Loches par un chemin peu connu de ceux de sa suite, le duc de Guise, qui se vantait de le savoir, se mit à la tête de la troupe pour servir de guide; mais, après avoir marché quelque temps, il s'égara et se trouva sur le bord d'une petite rivière qu'il ne reconnut pas lui-même. Le duc d'Anjou lui fit la guerre de les avoir si mal conduits et, étant arrêtés en ce lieu, aussi disposés à la joie qu'ont accoutumé de l'être de jeunes princes, ils aperçurent un petit bateau qui était arrêté au milieu de la rivière; et, comme elle n'était pas large, ils distinguèrent aisément dans ce bateau trois ou quatre femmes, et une entre autres qui leur sembla fort belle, qui était habillée magnifiquement, et qui regardait avec attention deux hommes qui pêchaient auprès d'elle. Cette aventure donna une nouvelle joie à ces jeunes princes et à tous ceux de leur suite. Elle leur parut une chose de roman. (P. 10)

In the pursuit of the *romanesque*, the hero and heroine are caught up in a web of intrigue and adventure, the culmination of which is the scene of the *rapt manqué* leading to a disheartening end, to the death of Mme de Montpensier. The irresistible trap of the myth of passion, the pursuit of "une chose de roman," the construction of their own *roman*, are swiftly and brutally destroyed by an author intent on abolishing an entire code, both moral and aesthetic. And with the exception of *Zaïde*, which conforms in structure and even theme far more to earlier traditions than to the "new novel" of Mme de Lafayette, all the tales point in the same direction. Illusions must be dismantled, and to do so, the transmitters of the illusions, the *précieux* novels, must be revealed as sham, for they are perhaps after all not the transmitters but rather the very creators of the myth. Their so-called verity must fall, and Mme de Lafayette, re-creating *romanesque* scenes in the middle of vast monotony and pain, successfully reveals the extent of their bankruptcy. And that is undoubtedly why her final work, *La Comtesse de Tende*, is charged with a strange intensity, with allusions to illegitimate pregnancy and birth, to great suffering, to a pathetic death. It stands as a most definitive slap at the "old way." The chimera is thus laid to rest.

1. Mme de Lafayette, *La Princesse de Montpensier* (Paris: Garnier Frères, 1970), p. 15. Subsequent references are to this edition, and will be found in the text. This method will also be followed for Mme de Lafayette's other works.

2. Georges Poulet, "Madame de Lafayette," in *Etudes sur le temps humain* (Paris: Plon, 1950), p. 122.

3. Mme de Lafayette, *La Princesse de Clèves* (Paris: Garnier Frères, 1970), p. 249.

4. Mme de Lafayette, *Zaïde* (Paris: Garnier Frères, 1970), p. 54.

5. Marie-Rose Carré, in "La Rencontre inachevée: étude sur la structure de *La Princesse de Clèves*," *PMLA* 87 (May 1972): 475-82, shows the importance of "seeing" in the novels. She concludes that for Mme de Lafayette the visual experience always excites but never satisfies.

6. An important exception to this conclusion is the study by Jules Brody, "*La Princesse de Clèves* and the Myth of Courtly Love," *University of Toronto Quarterly* 38 (January 1969): 105-35. Brody fully describes the erotic nature of the novel, insisting on the aggressive, sexual behavior of the duc de Nemours.

7. Jean Racine, *Phèdre* (Paris: Garnier Frères, 1960), act 1, scene 3, p. 547.

8. Michel Butor, "Sur 'La Princesse de Clèves,'" in *Répertoire* (Paris: Editions de Minuit, 1960), p. 76.

9. Bernard Pingaud, *Mme de Lafayette par elle-même* (Paris: Seuil, 1959), p. 90.

10. Mme de Lafayette, *La Comtesse de Tende* (Paris: Garnier Frères, 1970), p. 402.

11. Serge Doubrovsky, "*La Princesse de Clèves*: une interprétation existentielle," *Table ronde*, no. 138 (June 1959), p. 46.

12. René Descartes, *Les Passions de l'âme* (Paris: Gallimard, 1953), p. 66.

13. Ibid., p. 139.

14. Doubrovsky, "*La Princesse de Clèves*," p. 43.

15. Pingaud, *Mme de Lafayette par elle-même*, pp. 66-67.

16.  Marie-Jeanne Durry, *Madame de Lafayette* (Paris: Mercure de France, 1962), p. 14.

17.  Doubrovsky, "*La Princesse de Clèves*," p. 48.

18.  Gabriel Bounoure, "La Perle blanche," *Mercure de France*, no. 1213 (November 1964), p. 429.

Chapter Four

## SAINT-EVREMOND

AINT-EVREMOND'S WRITING experience is surely one of the most curious
among those of the moralists. His entire approach defies the classical rules of order,
structure, and impersonality. There is a strong
sense of the haphazard, an impression that comic and
serious can readily mingle, and, especially, a feeling that the
direct portrayal and analysis of the self are integrally a
part of writing. Moreover, Saint-Evremond attempts to
convey that he could just as soon not write as write, that
the act of writing is not always "serious"; sometimes, it is
only a game, an amusing pastime. How successfully he was
able to convince that he did indeed have the option of
silence is open to question. Ultimately it can be said that
his seeming nonchalance is little more than a pose, a means
to an ironic distance necessary to counteract any "over-
involvement," a means to emotional freedom.

There is also in Saint-Evremond a sense of disorder
that seems to be the outcome of a radically paradoxical
situation, set in motion by the confrontation between praise
of pleasure and fear of love. Both aspects of his stance
merit study, although the second part, his fear, has only
recently been fully understood.[1] Saint-Evremond's reticence
is complex, and the two diverging poles—involvement and

self-containment—not infrequently in the course of his writings pull together, then coincide, only to split apart once more.

There is, first, his heavy preoccupation with the concept of pleasure. As Victor Du Bled has shown, there were degrees of libertine thought in the seventeenth century, with Saint-Evremond situated definitely along a more moderate line,[2] always reluctant to relinquish a vocabulary of discernment, discretion, and moderation; nevertheless, his ideas follow a well-defined, carefully structured conception of pleasure, with the self and its well-being always at the center.

The underlying question that pervaded seventeenth-century French thought—"What shall man do to be saved?" —was the problem with which Saint-Evremond also was struggling. His answer was at antipodes from that of Pascal and the Jansenist writers. Christian faith, with its renouncement of worldly pleasure and its emphasis on the gift of grace, never seduced Saint-Evremond, except perhaps as an emotional strength that he occasionally envied, but always from a distance. Even more vehement than his questioning of abstinence to gain salvation, however, is his denigration of a life of metaphysical speculation, as embodied in the ideas of Descartes: "Je ne vis plus que par réflexion sur la vie, ce qui n'est pas proprement vivre; et sans la philosophie de M. Descartes qui dit: je pense donc je suis, je ne croirais pas proprement être."[3] But it was not only to experience more fully his own vitality that Saint-Evremond rejected the meditative, contemplative way of life. Interspersed throughout his works are frequent allusions to man's inability to understand the human condition, to his ultimate blindness in all matters of life and death, of body and soul. Thus to the eschatological debate of the time, already so deeply ingrained into the century's traditions, Saint-Evremond proposed a response radically different from that of either Descartes or the Jansenists: pleasure, here and now. *Le plaisir* is one of the primary words and themes of Saint-Evremond's

[74]

writings, and he tried over the years to create from it a true ideal, with an *art de vivre* to match.

The concept of pleasure in seventeenth-century thought was dominated by the Dutch philosopher Spinoza. Saint-Evremond sojourned twice in Holland, the first time in 1661 and 1662, only briefly, and again for a lengthy period of time, from 1665 to 1669, interrupting his exile in England. It is known that he met with Spinoza. But the question of influence is always a touchy one, and in this case, to create too close a kinship between men whose writing experiences differed so sharply—the Frenchman bordering on the *mondain* trend of the era, the Dutchman steeped in the greatest depths of philosophical examination—would be misleading.

Spinoza is one of the sternest, most demanding, least permissive of moralists, and he and Saint-Evremond are widely different. The Dutch philosopher, moreover, differs markedly from writers like Gassendi, who had a direct bearing upon Saint-Evremond's thought. Nevertheless, Spinoza's elaborate formulation of a "pleasure principle" seems to have guided Saint-Evremond, if not in a very substantial way, at least then as a preliminary direction. Of particular significance is the Dutch philosopher's recognition of the essential unity of things, his refusal to split the world into distinct substances, a belief, moreover, that the post-Freudian writers have seized upon:

> On the problem of human happiness, what distinguishes Spinoza from the Western philosophic tradition . . . is his allegiance to the pleasure-principle and his rejection of mind-body dualism. His allegiance to the pleasure-principle brings him to recognize the narcissistic, self-enjoying character of human desire, and hence to recognize that human perfection consists in an expansion of the self until it enjoys the world as it enjoys itself.[4]

Saint-Evremond, though shunning the "hard" consequences of much of Spinoza's thought, nevertheless makes use of these concepts of pleasure and fundamental unity.

There are several important ideas in the above selection,

[75]

not the least of which is the problem of mind-body dualism. The Jansenist writers faced the same dilemma, and their answer was most nearly consistent with centuries of Western tradition, both Christian and Platonic: the persistent denigration of the body. Saint-Evremond offered another solution. Although he was always careful to distinguish his particular brand of "volupté"—a general well-being and sense of fulfillment deriving from the *honnête* code—from any connotation of debauchery, nevertheless, true, bodily pleasure was an integral part of his world. His deep-riding sensuality is most directly and beautifully conveyed in his frequent praise of *la bonne chère*. Sensual pleasure was most intensely experienced through eating, and he relished descriptions of succulent fruits and full-bodied wines.

To eat is to feel alive; to detail one's intense enjoyment is to grant a high position to physical gratification. This is not to say that Saint-Evremond relied exclusively upon sensual gratification for achieving happiness. He was always quick to praise the mind's pleasures, too, and it was precisely in this drawing together of two traditionally contrary forces into a composite whole that Saint-Evremond achieved the ideal of both Epicurus and Spinoza. The physical and the spiritual need not exclude each other, as the devout Christian writers would have it. Rather, in the true style of *l'honnêteté*, they may be viewed as complementary forces in a harmonious, balanced life.

Saint-Evremond was fully cognizant of the potent human capacity for loving, a belief he expressed, nevertheless, with utmost discretion: "Il est certain que la nature a mis en nos coeurs quelque chose d'aimant (si on le peut dire), quelque principe secret d'affection, quelque fond caché de tendresse, qui s'explique et se rend communicable avec le temps."[5] The deliberately vague words, the almost *précieux* tone of the aphorism, cannot hide what Saint-Evremond is alluding to, precisely a "quantum" of affectionate energy, a "love force" that will reveal itself with time but also from underneath a vocabulary of reticence. In order best to develop this concept, Saint-Evremond leans heavily upon a basic life energy, essential to every human being and which will be augmented by love. His ideas on this subject are, however, expressed in a language charged with extraordinary egocentrism, and "love" in Saint-Evremond's moral universe reflects the growing awareness of "selfness" that permeates the age.

This is why Brown's passage on Spinoza is significant, in that it calls attention to extreme intensification of the self. In a more limited and more mundane fashion, for Saint-Evremond, too, the self and its pleasure are primary. To dwell as completely as he did on the pleasure motive within each individual was to say that the self and its gratification are the ultimate morality as well as the ultimate salvation. What he demanded, therefore, was a constant awareness that the individual conscience is sacrosanct, and that exterior, imposed standards should not stand in the way of man's pleasure. It is a highly egotistical stance (in a non-pejorative sense), fully in keeping with what Saint-Evremond sought to gain in the way toward an eventual self-liberation for all.

It is not surprising, therefore, that Saint-Evremond categorically shunned the family's authoritative moral norms that tended to go counter to individual needs. This was particularly so as these standards manifested themselves in the lives of the young women of the age, to whom he was a frequent "counselor." In a letter to one young female acquaintance, he resolutely advises against parental subjugation:

> Je ne doute point que l'entrevue de votre sainte Mère, et de toute votre pieuse Famille n'ait été accompagnée de beaucoup de pleurs. Vous aurez donné aux larmes de cette Mère des larmes civiles et respectueuses, comme une Fille bien née. . . . C'est assez d'avoir obéi une fois, et sacrifié votre repos à une complaisance, que peut-être vous ne lui deviez pas. . . . Elle est injuste, après avoir exigé de vous une si dure obéissance, de vouloir régler vos inclinations. . . . On aime ce qui plaît, et non point ce qui est permis.[6]

What Saint-Evremond envisioned was a free and independent spirit, capable of placing its pleasure above the demands of the family, which ran counter to self-fulfillment. The erotic force or energy that Saint-Evremond had perceived (although he always couched it in "discreet" language) demanded a freedom that the family, as the essential social unit, could not condone.

But the moral authority that the parent seeks to impose upon his children may be embodied within the spoken or unspoken tenets of the society, where it is perhaps even more potent than within the confines of the home. In the well-known letter Saint-Evremond addressed to Mlle de Quéroualle, who was being wooed by the English monarch Charles II, and who was supposedly torn by her wish to submit and her desire to maintain a chaste reputation, he urges her to become the king's mistress (for political reasons, too, perhaps, although these are unmentioned in the letter). Having weighed virtue against pleasure, he comes out strongly for the latter: "Heureuse qui peut se conduire discrètement sans gêner ses inclinations! car s'il y a de la honte à aimer sans retenue, il y a bien de la peine à passer la vie sans Amour. . . . Ne rebutez pas trop sévèrement les tentations en ce Pays-ci" (3:90). In his "decent" language, Saint-Evremond here clearly pits the moral dicta of society against the inner demands of the self, and the inclinations to which he most discreetly refers are precisely those of the body. Social authority, when in opposition to the individual's happiness, must be worn down. (It must also be said that there is a strong element of *voyeur* or "outsider" in the letters to female friends. When he freely offers them his advice, it seems almost as if his pleasure is in "confessing" them, in sharing their anguish in a somewhat paternalistic but distant fashion.)

What is needed, then, is a constant attention to all forces that act upon the individual, a weighing of their relative importance to his emotional state, and an eventual selection of those that will contribute the most to one's enjoyment, without passing the limits of a self-imposed code of decency and restraint, the mark of *l'honnête homme*. The love "quantum," that which Saint-Evremond called the "principe secret d'affection," is, viewed within this framework, nothing less than an intensification of life, potent in the ability to counteract obsession with death, to glorify the life force itself. Beyond that, however, it is that which is most intimately and integrally part of the "self," that which will most readily resist control by "outside" standards, and thus, for Saint-Evremond, the ultimate symbol of human freedom.

The act of selection requisite to this "sorting out" process demands not only an awareness and an understanding of the self but also a total immersion in an egocentric universe, whereas the "other" counts only as a force to be analyzed, reckoned with, selected or rejected. Erotic energy, the power of love, is thus easily convertible into a force of control, *l'honnête homme* or *l'honnête femme* stepping back from diverse emotional pulls if they threaten psychic disintegration. Thus, while counseling his women friends to reject imposed social standards, while urging them to seek the greatest freedom possible, he nevertheless remains fixed on the theme of control, which is central to the performance of man in society. Saint-Evremond's attitude is summed up in a letter to madame la duchesse de Mazarin, his longtime friend, written at a moment of particular difficulty in her life: "Faites revenir ce temps heureux, où toujours Maîtresse de vous-même, vous ne laissiez de liberté à personne qui valut la peine d'être assujettie" (4:210-11). This ready intermingling of love and power is perhaps more than anything else the mark of "la littérature de l'honnêteté," the sign also of the new priorities, Eros becoming a predominantly social force, in a world where the societal predominates.

In particular, however, it was obvious to Saint-Evremond that a philosophy, however non-structured in appearance, of pleasure, however modest, necessitated an absolute attention to the present. A belief in the full expression of the self demanded a total commitment to "now." Evaluat-

[79]

ing the moral weight to be attributed to past society versus present, Saint-Evremond was quick to establish the pre-eminence of the latter:

> Je sais que la Raison nous a été donnée pour régler nos Moeurs: mais la Raison, autrefois rude et austère, s'est civilisée avec le temps; elle ne conserve aujourd'hui presque rien de son ancienne rigidité. Il lui a fallu de l'austérité pour établir des Lois, qui pussent empêcher les Outrages et les Violences: elle s'est adoucie pour introduire l'Honnêteté dans le commerce des hommes, elle est devenue délicate et curieuse dans la recherche des Plaisirs, pour rendre la vie aussi agréable qu'on avait tâché de la rendre sûre et honnête. Ainsi, Monsieur, il faut oublier un temps, où c'était assez d'être sévère, pour être cru vertueux, puisque la Politesse, la Galanterie, la Science des voluptés, font une partie du Mérite présentement. (2:333)

There is no dream of another social structure more satisfying than the present one, and moral standards of the past cannot be made to apply to the present.

Within an individual life also, the past fails to offer substance. A past love, for Saint-Evremond, is a dead love; and conversely, a dead lover belongs only to the past. Exhorting Mme de Mazarin to quit her mourning for a lover who was killed—"les Amoureux sont mortels comme les autres" (4:193)—Saint-Evremond sought to achieve a realistic appraisal of time, placing all his value firmly in the present. Death should bring to those who live on, not obligation, but freedom; and the intense dedication to the self that Saint-Evremond preached did require an extraordinary facility of emotional disengagement, necessary to maintain the standards of control dictated by *l'honnêteté*.

He makes a parallel stand for the future. There is no question of an afterlife in his moral outlook, no balancing of present happiness against future salvation. Salvation is here, on earth. There is no Pascalian wager. The future is simply demystified. Nor is there any room for future regret, for guilt. Veiled or unveiled threats of hell are weak compared with the need for love, and should not be used as deterrents to the individual's needs: "La peur de la Damnation, l'image de l'Enfer avec tous ses feux, ne lui ôteront jamais l'idée d'un Amant" (4:277). For Saint-Evremond there is no mystical force to be reckoned with; there is only the strong feeling of strong passion, and thoughts of an afterlife, of possible damnation or salvation, are pushed aside and rejected.

The self-oriented, pleasure-seeking individual must, in addition, maintain an attitude of flexible "availability" and disengagement in his social contacts. Pleasure must never become tyranny or obsession. Again, it is a matter of the self controlling and manipulating outside forces to the end of its own happiness; hence, increasing the number of loves, the amount of loving, violates no code but only enhances the possibilities of fulfillment. The "quelque chose d'aimant" sets no limits upon its capacity for satisfaction, and thus Saint-Evremond rejects an over-attachment to any one person: "Se réduire à n'aimer qu'une personne, c'est se disposer à haïr toutes les autres: et ce qu'on croit une Vertu admirable à l'égard d'un Particulier, est un grand crime envers tout le Monde" (4:122). There is something monstrously antisocial in exclusivity, a crime against mankind. But it is more than that. He clearly saw the enormous danger to the individual's liberty in an over-attachment to the "other." This tyranny had to be avoided, and the self remain free to enter and leave relationships as necessary, the vital energy force protected against any encroachment. The emotional vigor must never be violated, the precarious equilibrium between pleasure and restraint remaining intact.

But it is particularly the question of infidelity that occupies Saint-Evremond when he speaks of pleasure and tyranny, and it is at this point that his *morale* goes most clearly and forcefully against traditional, established social standards. As "spiritual adviser" to a seemingly large group of women, Saint-Evremond did not hesitate to counsel freedom from attachments based on standardized norms or simply on time:

[81]

Il n'y a rien de si honnête qu'une ancienne Amitié, et rien de si honteux qu'une vieille Passion. Détrompez-vous du faux mérite d'être fidèle. . . .

Mais que d'ennuis accompagnent toujours cette misérable Vertu! Quelle différence des dégoûts de votre attachement à la délicatesse d'une Passion naissante! Dans une Passion nouvelle, vous trouverez toutes les heures délicieuses: les jours se passent à sentir de moment en moment qu'on aime mieux. Dans une vieille Habitude, le temps se consume ennuieusement à aimer moins. On peut vivre avec des Indifférents, ou par bienséance, ou par la nécessité du commerce: mais comment passer sa vie avec ceux qu'on a aimés, et qu'on n'aime plus? (1:96)

In the face of the established "virtues" of fidelity and commitment of a permanent nature, Saint-Evremond opted for the individual's chance to move freely within his social universe. In Holland particularly he found the women bound to rigid, fixed standards that kept them faithful to a first lover: "moitié par habitude, moitié par un sot honneur qu'on se fait d'être constant, on entretient languissamment les misérables restes d'une Passion usée" (2:232). Long tormented by the passage of time (which may well explain the peculiar game of "being old" he so expertly played, even in early middle age), Saint-Evremond rejected and shunned allegiances based upon accumulated days. A relationship whose sole foundation was one of habit was the very antithesis of his ideal rapport, where both partners enjoyed a sense of renewed vitality.

Up until now, it seems clear that Saint-Evremond was engaged, to a greater or lesser degree, in the moral dilemma of his age, of all ages. Where was man to find happiness? And how was he to build a life accordingly? Saint-Evremond's answer fits into a general schema of thought that traversed his century, heir to the skepticism and doubt engendered during the Renaissance. Most specifically, he questioned the Christian reliance upon future salvation, rejected it, and came forth with his answer of modified terrestrial pleasure. But his ideas are not bound into well-structured philosophical treatises, and it is more and more difficult to separate the man's own particular sensitivites from the "moral" he espoused, especially when he readily makes his person so available to us. Thus what on the one hand appears as an intellectual celebration of freedom from constraint is on the other only one man's special battle against pain, against obsession with death. And although the emphasis on the life forces was an integral part of the "libertine" philosophy of the time—indeed, almost a convention—bit by bit Saint-Evremond's words on the subject take on a surprisingly personal tone.

Unquestionably, a philosophy of terrestrial pleasure could not fail to be distressed by a certain end to that happiness. Or it may be that the obsession with death is the emotional fear that gives rise to the intellectual construct of earthly gratification. In any case, Saint-Evremond sought to allay the death fear by a very deliberate stress on life; and the belief in *disponibilité*, in the present time rather than in the past or future, in total self-determination, reflects an attempt at firmly rooting the individual in his immediate "selfdom." Actually, it is not the obsession with ultimate death alone that Saint-Evremond sought to diminish, but all the pain in life, all the little deaths that strip man of an essential feeling of well-being.

Among the critics, H. T. Barnwell in particular has done a thorough job of analyzing the question of *le divertissement* in the writings of Saint-Evremond, showing that the pleasure theory served as a potent counterforce to the fear of death and pain.[7] Pleasure, then, is seen as a way of attaining an emotional equilibrium that neither Christian grace nor rational meditation could offer. That is why the principle of self-fulfillment and self-enjoyment must be maintained at all cost, rising above obligations to one's family and society, why moral authority with its emphasis on what is "due" must be withered away, as a threat to the supremacy of individual determination.

The result of this attitude is much less an extolling of spectacular happiness than the calm acceptance of a *modus*

[83]

*vivendi,* where freedom from pain and fear is equated with genuine bliss. There was always within Saint-Evremond the realization that to achieve a complete, total joy, an omnipresent happiness, was a radical impossibility. At best one could hope for a compromise situation, where the absence of pain and unhappiness, the absence especially of the dominating fear of death, would allow for a satisfactory life situation. His parody of the *cogito*— "J'aime donc je suis"—is simply an affirmation of the desire for life weighted against all forms of pain, against meditation that leads to thoughts of ultimate nothingness. In this equivocal, ambiguous call to pleasure, Saint-Evremond's works begin to separate from the general, free-thinking current of his age and to assume their own unique quality.

The capacity to accept a compromise situation somewhere between joy and pain is why Saint-Evremond seems so willing, so eager, to replace love with friendship, to engage in a game where one is easily converted into the other, where the intense, vibrant feelings of passion can be readily interchanged with the calm felicity of friendship: "Et si je passe de l'Amitié à l'Amour sans emportement, je puis revenir de l'Amour à l'Amitié avec aussi peu de violence" (1:59). His pleasure was never frenzied but quiet, and the persistent image of the ugly, tired, old man, which he so frequently employed in self-description, served to support his need; for such an individual is beyond the love domain, exempt from Eros.

But of greatest significance for this study is the question of emotional risk. Clearly, the danger for potential psychic and social disintegration involved in friendship is far weaker than that associated with love. No great emotional turbulence is associated with friendship, traditionally, for the sexual component is absent, whereas *l'amour-passion,* perhaps more readily than any other force, can undo the stable network of the individual psyche and the collective society.

Thus the writer who counseled his many correspondents

[84]

(mostly female) to indulge in sensual enjoyment of the freest nature, who spoke with such feeling on the value of passion in one's life, ultimately bows to the conceptions of love that dominated his age. Friendship is the furthest point to which Saint-Evremond could comfortably adhere, and even at those times when he gives way to "amorous" sentiments (with Mme de Mazarin), his posture is pathetically submissive and placating—"Baisez le vieillard, Reine!" (4:112)—thus violating all the concepts of emotional independence and detachment he had so readily espoused. But even these supplications seem strangely devoid of emotion and serve only to disparage ironically his own self.

Love enticed him as a philosophical ideal, as the symbol of the pinnacle of pleasure, but he gladly yielded in favor of a less-demanding relationship. His emphasis on friendship did not violate his strong belief in pleasure, of course; the Epicurean ideal included all forms of physical and mental pleasures. But it did reduce the degree of desired emotional intensity. Even during the rare times that he analyzed the quality of love, Saint-Evremond was moved by that aspect which offered the smallest amount of emotional turbulence, by that which most successfully eliminated confusion of an erotic base:

> Quoique l'Amour agisse diversement selon la diversité des complexions, on peut rapporter à trois mouvements principaux tout ce que nous fait sentir une passion si générale: aimer, brûler, languir.
> Aimer simplement, est le premier état de notre Ame, lorsqu'elle s'émeut par l'impression de quelque objet agréable. . . . Brûler, est un état violent sujet aux inquiétudes, aux peines, aux tourments. . . . Languir, est le plus beau des mouvements de l'Amour; c'est l'effet délicat d'une flamme pure, qui nous confuse doucement. (3:123)

His praise goes for languishing, because Saint-Evremond shunned the tumultuous aspect of love as too upsetting to a precarious emotional well-being. He enjoyed best a feeling of calm and repose, that same feeling he obtained from a steady but undemanding friendship, free from the intense, anxious side of passionate love. He often admitted that he would have enjoyed a friendship with a woman if the relationship could have remained unhampered by agitated, sexual feelings.

But it is perhaps in his attitude toward women that Saint-Evremond shifts most obviously between two different standards: the philosophical glorification of love and the personal fear. Women troubled him. He liked to point out that some of the most famous men in history lived independently of female company, and he even offered a short praise of homosexuality, unusual for his time, as a viable alternative to heterosexual love (4:115). But the female character persistently disturbed him, at least as he reveals those anxieties in his writings, and he seems to have been most relaxed toward women when they were not a part of his own life.

Resolutely pro-Nature when advising female friends, although somewhat distant and removed, Saint-Evremond lashed out against prudery in all forms. In the letter to Mlle de Quéroualle, he wrote: "Mais vous savez trop le Monde, pour donner de véritables tendresses aux chagrins des Prudes, dont la Vertu n'est qu'un artifice pour vous priver des plaisirs qu'elles regrettent" (1:90). Prudery for Saint-Evremond, as for Molière, was little else than a mask, a poor travesty for women unlucky enough to be deprived of lovers, camouflaging their bitterness under a blanket of virtue.

For the same reason, he was quick to condemn convent life, where love blooms rather than fades away, where erotic love, or at least the desire for it, surfaces quickly: "Au lieu de porter au Couvent le dégoût de l'Amour, le Couvent vous en fera naître l'envie. . . . Ainsi vous serez consumée de regrets, ou dévorée de désirs, selon que votre Ame se tournera au souvenir de ce que vous avez pu faire, ou à l'imagination de ce que vous ne pourrez exécuter" (3:92). The inevitable result, according to Saint-Evremond, is that passion is converted into religious devotion, and God becomes a new lover (1:137).

He attacked equally vigorously *les précieuses*, whom he saw as violating the laws of Nature as severely as the prudes. What he recognized in their overly intellectual approach to love is what modern critics have referred to as their sublimation of passion. "Les Jansénistes de l'Amour," as he chose to call them, adopting the expression from Ninon de Lenclos, violated the very foundation of passion by denying its affective power: "Elles ont tiré une Passion toute sensible du Coeur à l'Esprit, et converti des mouvements en Idées" (1:111). This intellectualization and deification of love go contrary to Saint-Evremond's belief in sensual gratification and its "here and now" quality. Any cult of love was repugnant to him, which is undoubtedly why, along with his attack on the *précieuses*, he also criticized the vestiges of *la courtoisie* in seventeenth-century Spanish mores. Love considered as a game, with set rules to follow, was for Saint-Evremond a basic denial of natural instinct. This attitude, however, did not prevent him from writing what must surely be some of the tritest love poetry of the *précieux* genre, but he saw that as strictly an exercise in style and not as a code of living.

Nevertheless, though vociferously defending Nature's way, though attacking multifold inhibitions and obstacles, Saint-Evremond's own portrayal of the ideal woman and the ideal love is a masterpiece of the very bias he so angrily denounced. In fact, this "portrait" reveals itself as the summation of Saint-Evremond's double stance— the fascination with love and the equally strong fear of it. The title of the passage alone serves to suggest a most fanciful, ephemeral situation: "Idée de la femme qui ne se trouve point, et qui ne se trouvera jamais." The non-existence of such a woman is thereby established before Saint-Evremond has even begun the body of the text, and the entire essay is built upon a series of antitheses whose member elements cancel out one another:

Sa Taille est d'une juste grandeur, bien prise, aisée, d'un dégagement aussi éloigné de la contrainte, que de cette excessive liberté. . . . Son Esprit a de l'étendue, sans être vaste, n'allant jamais si loin dans les pensées générales, qu'il ne puisse revenir aux considérations particulières. . . . [Elle est] également ennemie d'un mouvement inutile, et de la mollesse d'un repos, qui se fait honneur du nom de Tranquillité, pour couvrir une véritable Nonchalance. (2:243-45)

Saint-Evremond's ideal female is an equilibrium of contrasting components, whose parts he manipulates back and forth until the whole self disappears in a display of verbiage that negates rather than creates.

But the most striking sets of contrasts are those that describe Emilie's prowess as a woman:

Elle vous attire, elle vous retient, et vous approchez toujours d'elle avec des désirs que vous n'oseriez faire paraître. . . . On connaît par une infinité d'expériences, que l'Esprit s'aveugle en aimant; et l'Amour n'a presque jamais bien établi son pouvoir qu'après avoir ruiné celui de notre Raison. Sur le sujet d'Emilie, nos Sentiments deviennent plus passionnés, à mesure que nos Lumières sont plus épurées; et la Passion, qui a toujours paru une marque de Folie, est ici le plus véritable effet de notre bon sens. (2:245-46)

To counteract the fear of loss of reasoning powers, Saint-Evremond proposes a "new" passion, one where sensuality is increased through some vague, spiritual enlightenment, and vice versa. Unable or unwilling to consider ideal love as preeminently or even partially sexual, Saint-Evremond does not offer only the standard coupling of Love and Reason, but rather the intermingling of the two, their interpenetration. And ultimately it is the erotic that emerges as "purified," whereas the gains for Reason are far less clear, for it was the former, always, that had been the disturbing element.

Emilie attracts at the same time that she repels. There is a hint of sexuality, but it is quickly dispelled as the "purifying light" of reason takes over. Ultimately, Saint-Evremond's ideal emotional experience involved a suspension of the faculties of deep feeling, and the most he can propose is a vocabulary of sensual expression, nullified by a contingent one of reason, sense, and purity. In light of this, it seems fair to suggest that the experience of Saint-Evremond was grounded in failure, that the "libertine" atmosphere of which he was decidedly a part, with its emphasis on physical pleasure, never succeeded in totally destroying the strong inhibitory forces that were part of the entire generation.

1. Leonard A. Rosmarin, "The Unsublimated Libido: Saint-Evremond's Conception of Love," *French Review* 46 (December 1972): 263-70.

2. Victor Du Bled, *La Société française du XVI$^e$ siècle au XX$^e$ siècle* (Paris: Perrin et Cie, 1904), 4th ser. (seventeenth century), p. 172.

3. Saint-Evremond, *Lettres*, ed. René Ternois, 2 vols. (Paris: Librairie Marcel Didier, 1967-68), 1:204.

4. Norman O. Brown, *Life against Death* (Middletown, Conn.: Wesleyan University Press, 1959), p. 47.

5. Rosmarin, "The Unsublimated Libido," p. 264.

6. Saint-Evremond, *Oeuvres*, 7 vols. (London: Tonson, 1711), 1:90. Subsequent references are to this edition, and will be found in the text.

7. H. T. Barnwell, *Les Idées morales et critiques de Saint-Evremond* (Paris: Presses universitaires de France, 1957), pp. 65-67.

Chapter Five

# MADAME DE SÉVIGNÉ

"ELLE N'A PAS DE PASSION AU COEUR en écrivant: mettons à part toujours l'amour maternel."[1] Gustave Lanson's earnest desire to relegate Mme de Sévigné's passion for her daughter to a substrate level reflects his basic preoccupation with the nonessential side of the voluminous correspondence. Lanson was most fascinated by the anecdotal Mme de Sévigné, the part of the letters given over to describing the multifold events of the time—"Toutes ces anecdotes, ces narrations charmantes ou poignantes, sont un des documents les plus sincères que l'histoire puisse consulter"[2]—and the ambiguous, strange relationship with Mme de Grignan is seen basically as an *écart* from the epistolary norm.

Certainly, Lanson's taste seems to have fixed Mme de Sévigné and her letters into a mold that only recently has been deemed questionable. Most of the *morceaux choisis* collections refer constantly to the letters depicting the death of Turenne, the representation of Racine's *Esther*, and, suspecting perhaps that it was at least necessary to allude once to the feelings of Mme de Sévigné for Mme de Grignan, the editors frequently include the famous episode of the crossing of the Avignon bridge. Seemingly, one reason for easily including the latter piece would be that stylistically, through its reenactment of the little drama, it conforms to the general notion we have of Mme de Sévigné as a tableau painter, gifted in depicting a certain sense of color and movement through the written word.

But in the past few years, critical interpretations have centered on the primary, essential point of the correspondence: the mother-daughter relationship. Reading through the three volumes of the letters in the Pléiade edition, it is evident immediately that the anecdotal approach is more than merely limiting. Such analysis actually disfigures the work, for the anecdote serves only as a support, or even sometimes as a foil, for the one element that overwhelmingly dominates the letters to Mme de Grignan—the expression of the great love.

In terms of the general study I have proposed, it is fair to question whether the letters occupy the same position toward society as the works of the other writers. Do they offer a general view of man in his universe—both immediate and cosmic? Do they propose a code or style of living? Does the introduction of "je" alter the basic intention of the seventeenth-century moralists: an impersonal negating and subsequent reconstruction of social patterns most necessary to the fundamental well-being of the individual and his society? In reply it must be said that a very powerful view of life, of living, does emerge from the letters of Mme de Sévigné; and in fact, it is one that goes counter to the philosophical and religious thinking of the day. Mme de Sévigné identified living with loving.

The Jansenist, Epicurean, and *mondain* codes are all violated by this other life-view: Jansenism by Mme de Sévigné's heavy emphasis on human love; Epicureanism by her willingness to plunge into a total, highly intense involvement with another, thereby sacrificing repose and emotional liberty; and finally *la mondanité* by her refusal to establish an idiom allowing for the superficial transfer of sentiment without loss of inner control. Unlike the great majority of classical moralists, Mme de Sévigné opted, through her letters, for a radical approach to life, radical in that it embraced the passions without fear.

[92]

Nevertheless, her stance is not without ambiguity. Life as love is not exactly what Mme de Sévigné chose, or it is precisely what she chose if living can be completely synonymous with writing. There is a distinction between stressing her passion or stressing the writing that interpreted it, between Mme de Sévigné primarily as active "lover" or passive poet. Recent criticism has tended to emphasize one side at the expense of the other, sometimes forgetting that the feelings and their expression can be separated only with great difficulty. Roger Duchêne in his *Madame de Sévigné et la lettre d'amour* accentuates her passion as a living force, so strong that she had to express it constantly. Left without any other means to do so, she opted for the letter. His study traces the history of Mme de Sévigné's passionate love for Mme de Grignan. Letter-writing is seen as a means to filling in the terrible gap that Mme de Grignan's departure for Provence had created. Beginning with the fateful day, Duchêne skillfully follows the life of Mme de Sévigné's unusually intense love: "Les lettres à Mme de Grignan permettent de suivre les étapes de l'évolution des sentiments de Mme de Sévigné. Après les lents progrès vers une meilleure entente de 1671 à 1676, vient la brusque rupture de 1677 avec, jusqu'en 1680, des sursauts et des paroxysmes. Et c'est enfin, dans une sérénité un peu grave, l'accord que seule attriste la pensée de la mort. La preuve de la vérité de l'amour dans les lettres, c'est cette courbe, dessinée au jour le jour, d'une affection s'étalant sur vingt-cinq années."[3]

Whereas Duchêne is interested primarily in the curve of Mme de Sévigné's love for her daughter and in examining the reasons for such fluctuation, Gérard-Gailly, in his introduction to the Pléiade edition of the letters, offers a Freudian analysis of the passion itself. Duchêne describes from the outside; Gérard-Gailly from the inside. His reading centers primarily upon certain semi-erotic passages of the letters and he concludes: "Passion maternelle! Maternelle, sans doute, mais amoureuse aussi, et passion d'amant pour un autre être humain."[4] His views are reinforced by the fact that the more obvious "love" passages were re-

moved by Mme de Sévigné's earliest editors, who probably recognized their ambiguous value.

For other critics, notably Jean Cordelier, the love relationship between Mme de Sévigné and Mme de Grignan
is viewed as the means through which the former was best
able to fulfill a calling as a writer. Cordelier seeks to prove
that the passion she experienced was only indirectly tied
to Mme de Grignan, via the necessity of writing. Thus she
loved the person who allowed her to realize her vocation.[5]
Interpreting the question of language in a different vein,
Bernard Bray explains that the erotic language Mme de
Sévigné frequently used in the letters to her daughter was
the result of a linguistic impasse. She was forced into the
lyric note because "la marquise ne disposait d'aucun
autre langage pour exprimer la douleur de l'absence."[6]
This interpretation is diametrically opposed to the Freudian
analysis of Gérard-Gailly, and the center of focus shifts
from the psychological to the socio-linguistic.

All the methods used to analyze the correspondence
both succeed and fail in their attempts to understand the
strange letters. Roger Duchêne's exhaustive study maintains
too strict a parallel between living and writing. He is so
interested in the gaps between letters, in what mother and
daughter were feeling at all times, that he forgets that Mme
de Sévigné's primary identity is through letter-writing,
and hence through the domain of the summary, the deliberate exclusion, not through any consecutive, all-inclusive
pattern.

As for Gérard-Gailly's Freudian study, it too fails at a
certain point. Without a doubt his perceptions do open
doors, for very frequently Mme de Sévigné's "maternal"
love appears ambiguous. The rivalry with M. de Grignan
for control over her daughter, the fascination with Mme de
Grignan's physical beauty, the references to kisses and
embraces far beyond polite convention, point to a situation
that seemingly reflects desires of incest and sapphism.
Mme de Sévigné herself, on occasion, found it useful to
clarify that her love was *maternel,* as if other thoughts had

indeed crossed her mind at some point. But the Freudian bent ultimately fails to tell the whole story, for the letters show that writing was a clear alternative—in fact, even sometimes a clear preference—to physical presence, and their love seemed to express itself most satisfactorily for both parties when the written word could interpret it. Thus a study of psyches and motives cannot reflect the entire problem, for it neglects the very crucial question of the necessity to remain in the domain of written communication, and, going one step further, in the domain of the imagination.

On the other hand, the theories stressing the writing experience are belied by Mme de Sévigné herself. Although in reality her great passion may have fared far better when on paper than at any other time, she nevertheless did believe that writing was a substitute for Mme de Grignan's presence, that it was only second best: "Quand je ne suis pas avec vous, mon unique divertissement est de vous écrire" (1:611). On the conscious plane, the marquise perceived that seeing was highly desirable, and writing, a palliative. Thus Jean Cordelier's neat little system transforming "je vivrai pour vous aimer" into "je vivrai pour vous écrire"[7] stretches the truth. That writing emerges eventually as a superior alternative to being together is clear through the letters, but only at rare moments was it viewed as such by Mme de Sévigné. Most of the time, she yearned for her daughter's presence. Finally, Bernard Bray, in emphasizing that linguistic patterns alone dictated Mme de Sévigné's expression, cannot sufficiently take into account either the nature of the relationship or the view of living that Mme de Sévigné sought to communicate. Ultimately, all aspects involved in Mme de Sévigné's relationship with her daughter must be studied, not only the fundamental ties but also how and why this alliance expressed itself as it did.

It is difficult to ascertain the precise nature of Mme de Sévigné's feeling for her daughter prior to the latter's departure for Provence, shortly after her marriage. In the face of scholarship suggesting that Mme de Sévigné's love for her daughter was an outgrowth only of Mme de Grignan's marriage and subsequent departure, and thus of a loss of a person who for so many years had been dominated and dependent, other critics have attempted to show that the separation of the two women marked only a heightening of an already forceful passion.[8]

There is really no strong evidence either way. But does an understanding of the years that preceded the 1671 departure to Provence shed much light on the correspondence itself? The only important question—that of Mme de Sévigné's possible desire to dominate her child—can be gleaned readily through the letters themselves, and references to past patterns of behavior do little to clarify that problem. However, by no means was the dependence-independence syndrome the sole, or even primary, reason for Mme de Sévigné's faithful correspondence, a view that might be suggested by an overly detailed account of the years previous to Mme de Grignan's departure.

What is significant is that the departure of Mme de Grignan for Provence on 5 February 1671 (where she was to follow her husband, who had just been named *lieutenant-général* by the court) was an abrupt move and a shock that was to release an expression of intense passion that, during the *grand siècle*, was paralleled perhaps only by the *Lettres portugaises*. The opening words of the first letter, written on 6 February 1671, one day after saying farewell to Mme de Grignan, set the note and tone of the twenty-five years of correspondence:

> Ma douleur serait bien médiocre si je pouvais vous la dépeindre; je ne l'entreprendrai pas aussi. J'ai beau chercher ma chère fille, je ne la trouve plus, et tous les pas qu'elle fait l'éloignent de moi. Je m'en allai donc à Sainte-Marie, toujours pleurant et toujours mourant: il me semblait qu'on m'arrachait le coeur et l'âme; et en effet, quelle rude séparation! (1:189)

Each subsequent separation following a period of re-union evokes a similar outcry; and although as she becomes

accustomed to the absence of her daughter Mme de Sévigné consciously attempts to modify her acute misery and
to modulate her tone, the letters are nevertheless, with
varying degrees of intensity, primarily the vivid expression of the anguish engendered by the "eternal" separation.
Through a process of *défiguration* that a collection of letters such as these cannot help but create, the reader is
left with the impression that the periods of separation far
surpassed in length the number of days when the two wom-
en were reunited. It is, however, the reverse that is true;
sixteen years, nine months together, eight years, four
months apart.[9] But it is not time together or apart, more
of one than of the other, that is really at stake here. The
nature of the feeling was such that each period of separation seemed "forever" to Mme de Sévigné.

The motives governing Mme de Sévigné's correspondence
with her daughter are no clearer than the precise nature of
their relationship prior to 1671. At times it appears that
the marquise was "engaged in a battle for a resisting
heart,"[10] that she sought to maintain her daughter in a
state of dependency inconsistent with the newly acquired
freedom that marriage and distance had bestowed upon Mme
de Grignan. Her frequently haughty, commanding tones
suggest that this was at least partially responsible for the
highly intense exchange of letters. At certain times—for
example, when she unsuccessfully exhorts Mme de Grignan
to join her at Vichy and then to return to Paris together
for the remainder of the year—it is obvious that a battle of
wills was a definite part of their relationship.

In a variation of the above theme, it could be postulated
that Mme de Sévigné's obsessive passion for Mme de
Grignan illustrates perfectly the fascination with an
"absent" person, the fascination that Proust described at
such length. Thus Mme de Grignan represents the creature
who ultimately escapes total possession, what Albertine
was for the *narrateur* of the *Recherche*. "Passion prou-
stienne, non pas que la mère de Mme de Grignan ait rien
d'une femme damnée . . . mais parce que son aventure
apparaît comme l'illustration parfaite de l'analyse que

[97]

Proust fera de la passion amoureuse, analyse qu'une brève citation de la *Recherche* suffit à rappeler: 'On n'aime que ce qu'on ne possède pas tout entier.' "[11] In this case, Françoise-Marguerite's portrait, which Mme de Sévigné keeps close to her throughout the years and to which she makes frequent reference in her letters, would be the perfect symbol of *l'être de fuite*, she who is both present and absent, the ideal metaphor for possession and lack of it.

But if precise motivation cannot be determined (for doubtless Mme de Sévigné was moved to write by several reasons), other questions can be more readily resolved. Reading through the letters consecutively, one perceives two important points: (1) the letters to Mme de Grignan do not fit in at all with the ongoing trends of *la mondanité* and *la galanterie*; and (2) on the writing level at least, Mme de Sévigné's involvement with her daughter was strikingly absolute and total.

That the marquise's relationship with Mme de Grignan, as she expressed it in her letters, far transcends any notions of simple gallantry or artificial social structures has been most thoroughly documented by Roger Duchêne in his recent comprehensive study of the letters. *La lettre galante* enjoyed much favor in seventeenth-century French society, where the salon life cultivated various socially acceptable "masks." Thus it emerges as an extremely well-perfected means to avoid the more fundamental sentiments of a primarily erotic base. "Parler d'amour s'avère en conséquence à la fois nécessaire et impossible, sauf précisément par le biais de la galanterie, masque commode et qui permet d'oser beaucoup puisqu'elle est réputée jeu d'esprit innocent, admis et même recommandé par les conventions de la vie mondaine."[12]

Such a code is evident in the letters of the marquise, although not in those to her daughter. Rather, it is in her correspondence with her male admirers that she readily introduces *la galanterie*, particularly in that addressed to Ménage and to Bussy-Rabutin, her cousin. Those letters are filled with wit and teasing grace, with joking ambiguities and puns. Especially in the letters to her cousin, Mme de Sévigné demonstrates a proclivity for a certain equivocal note, where frequent references of a sexual nature contrast with her very restrained, indignant manner when her cousin, provoked by her banter, steps beyond social rules. In the correspondence with her cousin, up until 1658 (in later years this tone is wholly absent from their commerce), the young marquise employs an art of adept word manipulation with great flair, referring to Bussy-Rabutin once, for example, he who had produced no sons, as "le beau faiseur des filles" (1:99).

The letters addressed to her daughter never joke about love or passion. Of course, Mme de Sévigné was writing then to someone of her own sex, and even if latent incestuous desires were present, the male-female element was absent. Hence there is an immediate reduction in any form of *la coquetterie.* But whereas quarrels or misunderstandings with Bussy-Rabutin or Ménage gave rise to a semi-serious, semi-teasing lilt, any disagreement between Mme de Grignan and her mother was a constant source of pain and bitterness. "Les rapports de la mère et de la fille," writes Jean Cordelier,

> ont tout d'une véritable liaison amoureuse: craintes sans fondement, jalousie sans cause, ergotages tendres, accusations aussi maladroites que sincères, protestations indignées, qui font de la *Correspondance* un chef-d'oeuvre de correspondance amoureuse, digne de figurer en bonne place dans toutes les anthologies de lettres d'amour.[13]

Mutual jealousy did indeed exert a strong influence throughout the letters—Mme de Sévigné's envy of Grignan; Françoise-Marguerite's antipathy toward Retz and Corbinelli, close friends and confidants of the marquise. Mme de Sévigné persistently lashed out at M. de Grignan, feeling that it was indeed her right to regulate even when he slept with his wife, to say nothing of the visits to Paris. The letters suggest, on the other hand, that Mme de Grignan was tormented by worry over her mother's "fidelity":

Avez-vous bien peur que j'aime mieux Mme de Brissac
que vous? Craignez-vous, de la manière dont vous me con-
naissez, que ses manières me plaisent plus que les vôtres?
que son esprit ait trouvé le chemin de me plaire? Avez-vous
opinion que sa beauté efface vos charmes? Enfin pensez-
vous qu'il y ait quelqu'un au monde qui puisse, à mon goût,
surpasser Madame de Grignan, étant même dépouillée de
tout l'intérêt que j'y prends? (1:265-66)

In the opposite vein, there were moments of great tenderness—Mme de Sévigné's pleas to her daughter to take
better care of her health; the frequent self-denigration
("j'ai trouvé mille fois que je ne valais pas l'extrême peine
que vous preniez pour moi" [2:259]) that alternated with
periods of frenzied worry when letters failed to arrive on
time or when the marquise believed that Mme de Grignan
was somehow in danger, anguish that was frequently without cause. Mme de Sévigné's imagination, her almost
masochistic pleasure in torturing herself by creating
dreaded adventures, demonstrate that the mood of the letters cannot compare with the cajoling, teasing tone of the
correspondence with Ménage and Bussy. Mme de Sévigné's letters to her daughter testify to an overwhelming
absorption, which had nothing in common with the orches-
trations of *la galanterie*.

Time after time, the marquise writes that her love, her
obsession, for her daughter, is in a realm separate from any
other domain of her life. To permit the development of
such emotion, to allow the feelings to attain a purer state,
she frequently sought out absolute solitude:

Quoique ma lettre soit datée du dimanche, je l'écris aujourd'hui, samedi au soir; il n'est que dix heures, tout est
retiré; c'est une heure où je suis à vous d'une manière plus
particulière qu'au milieu de ce qui est ordinairement dans
ma chambre: ce n'est pas que je sois contrainte, je sais me
débarrasser; je me promène seule, et quoi que vous disiez,
ma très chère, je serais bien oppressée si je n'avais pas cette
liberté. J'ai besoin de penser à vous avec attention, comme
j'avais besoin de vous voir. (3:18-19)

[100]

Solitude, however, necessarily depended upon the absence not only of all who were irrelevant to the passion but also of *l'objet aimé*. Doubtless, a certain amount of fictionalization occurred. What the solitude and the free reign of the imagination offered was the preferred formulation of her sentiments. Being alone allowed for the satisfaction of both the emotional need (constant attention focused on Mme de Grignan) and of the artistic one (perfection of the means of expression). Either way, what is important is the desire to isolate in order to concentrate best on the obsession to the exclusion of all else.

Countless times throughout the long period from 1671 to 1696, Mme de Sévigné explicitly states the degree to which the passion possesses her:

> Enfin tout tourne ou sur vous, ou de vous, ou pour vous, ou par vous. (1:235)

> Je vivrai pour vous aimer, et j'abandonne ma vie à cette occupation. (1:283)

> C'est une chose étrange que d'aimer autant que je vous aime: on a une attention et une application naturelle et continuelle, qui fait qu'en nulle heure du jour on ne peut être surprise sans cette pensée. (1:685-86)

> Quelle possession vous avez prise de mon coeur, et quelles traces vous avez faites dans ma tête! (2:454)

> Je pense continuellement et habituellement à vous. (2:460)

> Mon coeur est à vous . . . tout vous y cède et vous y laisse régner souverainement. (3:10)

Even the infrequent recourse to *précieux* expression—as in the last example—cannot detract from the totality of involvement that left little room for other emotional demands. The preoccupation with Mme de Grignan, or perhaps more precisely with the image of Mme de Grignan, the almost deification of that image, is one of the most remarkable aspects of the entire correspondence. One perceives that the extreme concentration upon her daughter, the quasi-religious fervor with which she endows the other woman's very being, was fundamentally vital to Mme de Sévigné, that this extraordinary effort and immersion was linked to the life flow.

Consciousness of her own body was very much a part of the marquise's passion. The love for her daughter is repeatedly tied to her own respiration—"Je souhaite, ma petite, que vous m'aimiez toujours: c'est ma vie, c'est l'air que je respire" (1:264)—and she "experienced it as consubstantial with her being, with her own identity."[14] What the mail brings and takes away is life itself. As Harriet Ray Allentuch has shown in her study, separation was seen as a period of mourning, of physical pain: "Cette séparation me fait une douleur au coeur et à l'âme, que je sens comme un mal du corps" (1:201).[15] Reunion, on the other hand, was viewed as spiritual and physical rebirth: "Quel voyage, bon Dieu! et quelle saison! vous arriverez précisément le plus court jour de l'année, et par conséquent vous nous ramenez le soleil" (2:259).[16]

In this identification of her love with the life process itself, Mme de Sévigné violates the precepts offered by the Jansenists, the Epicureans, and the *mondain* writers, all of whom placed another ideal—love of God, ataraxia, social perfection—above the intense emotional involvement absolutely vital to the marquise's sense of well-being. Even if, in part, the recourse to letter-writing reveals a decided preference for an attachment to what is absent, rather than a predilection for a permanent, "present" relationship, (a second marriage, perhaps), the commitment is nonetheless, of a different nature from those proposed by the other writers of the age.

The totality of the involvement, however, created certain problems, the most significant of which is the degree to which Mme de Sévigné altered reality—consciously or subconsciously—to conform to her emotional demands. Time, space, people, all undergo a radical transformation within the context of the letter.

[102]

The present is a nonexistent moment in the marquise's writings to her daughter. The passage of time is viewed within her own special confines, dependent upon her own private relativity:

> Pour cette négligence et cette joie de voir passer les jours les uns après les autres, je la sens en moi et j'y fais réflexion à toute heure. Quand vous êtes ici, il n'y en a pas un que je ne regrette; je trouve qu'ils m'échappent avec une vitesse qui m'attriste. Une heure, un jour, une semaine, un mois, un an, tout cela court et s'enfuit avec une rapidité qui m'afflige toujours. . . . . Présentement, ma bonne, que je ne respire que de vous revoir et vous pouvoir garder et conserver moi-même, je voudrais que tout cet intervalle fût passé; je jette les jours à la tête de qui les veut, je les remercie d'être passés. Le printemps et l'été encore me paraissent des siècles; il me semble que je n'en verrai jamais la fin. Je dors vite; et j'ai de l'impatience d'être toujours à demain, et puis de recevoir vos lettres, et puis d'en recevoir encore, et encore d'autres. (2:572-73)

But more is involved than simply an art of eloquent expression; for Mme de Sévigné the present assumes form and meaning only in relation to the past or the future, and is colored completely by either remorse or anticipation. Particularly in the earlier letters to Mme de Grignan, the ones written between 1671 and 1676, she alludes frequently to such states of mind. Thoughts that revolve upon the past are inevitably filled with great sadness of time lost: "Hélas! c'est ma folie que de vous voir, de vous parler, de vous entendre; je me dévore de cette envie, et du déplaisir de ne vous avoir pas assez écoutée, pas assez regardée" (1:230-31). She turns next to the future, since the past has not fulfilled and the present is suspended, a non-moment: "Il faut pourtant que je vous dise encore que je regarde le temps où je vous verrai comme le seul que je désire à présent et qui peut m'être agréable dans la vie" (1:282). And in one remarkable passage, written four years later, she shows with what ease she could make the transition from past to future, completely

[103]

negating the present: "Il est vrai que, depuis trois ans, nous n'avons été que quatre mois séparées, et ce qui s'est passé depuis votre départ. J'ai senti toute la joie de passer les étés et les hivers avec vous; et je sens encore plus le déplaisir de voir ce temps passé, et passé pour jamais, cela fait mourir. Il faut mettre à la place de cette pensée l'espérance de se revoir" (1:768-69).

The future reveals itself also as the undisputed answer to all problems, and, in fact, as a strong counterforce to a reality that is not only unsatisfying but frequently bitter. Even after a period of reunion that was particularly acrimonious, the future assumes a rosy glow, as Mme de Sévigné almost desperately invests time with qualities of transfiguration. The most recent reunion may have been a disaster, but time alone will change that, installing a reign of "truth" that the past has failed to achieve: "Eh, mon Dieu, ne nous reverrons-nous jamais en nous faisant sentir toutes les douceurs de l'amitié que nous avons? . . . Faisons donc mieux, ma bonne, une autre fois . . . faisons-nous honneur de nos sentiments, qui sont si beaux et si bons: pourquoi les défigurer" (2:280)? The problem, of course, lies in determining whether the reunion (in this case, unsuccessful) or the promise of another encounter (judged successful in advance) is the disfiguration of the truth. Living versus writing. The essential truth of the relationship, as Mme de Sévigné saw it, was revealed through the letters. That which did not adhere to the image was somehow inaccurate, false, *défiguré*.

Space, too, acquires new perspectives. That which is "dead" is really most alive. Through the resuscitative powers of memory, places that have a particularly strong association with Mme de Grignan and the past are those sites that most powerfully live within the marquise: "Il n'y a point d'endroit, point de lieu, ni dans la maison, ni dans l'église, ni dans le pays, ni dans le jardin, où je ne vous aie vue; il n'y en a point qui ne me fasse souvenir de quelque chose de quelque manière que ce soit; et de quelque façon que ce soit aussi, cela me perce le coeur. Je vous vois; vous m'êtes présente" (1:236).

[104]

But letter-writing achieves an even stronger transformation of reality. It was necessary, of course, in the correspondence with Mme de Grignan, to have recourse to the outside world, that is, to the world beyond Mme de Sévigné and her daughter. But did the marquise's references truly reflect ongoing reality? On a double level, it appears that by her particular selection of those to be mentioned in her letters, she conferred identity, existence even, to a choice few alone, and that her choice was ultimately guided by her passion for her daughter. As Bernard Bray has shown, the correspondence is a closed work, a perfect reflection of the closed society at its root; and the letters refer constantly to the same basic group of friends, acquaintances, and family, common to both Mme de Sévigné and Mme de Grignan.[17]

And yet the distinction of who enjoys favor—naming—does not stop there. Particularly those friends who are most deeply involved with Mme de Grignan—or who at least give that appearance to her mother—are included in the letters. Mme de Sévigné attempted to render her passion a collective one, to give it a sense of social primacy that it did not, could not, have. She sought to extricate her obsession from the strictly individual by endowing it with qualities of communal preoccupation: "Si je vous disais tous ceux qui vous font des compliments, il faudrait un volume: M. et Mme de Chaulnes, M. de Lavardin, M. le comte des Chapelles, Tonquedec, l'abbé de Montigny, évêque de Léon, M. d'Harouys cinq cent mille fois, Jean Fourché, Chésières, etc." (1:373). Those who refrained from such compliments were far less often alluded to, for Mme de Sévigné transformed the world according to her own highly limited standards.

This is the problem central to the correspondence, and one that at times did not escape Mme de Sévigné herself. Which is "more real"? Living or writing? Furthermore, is it through writing or being together that a more satisfactory version (vision) of life emerges? Although constantly seeking her daughter's presence, on a conscious level at least, as that which would achieve the greatest fulfillment for herself, Mme de Sévigné, on perhaps a deeper plane, was aware that letter-writing offered a viable and perhaps more sustaining alternative to living together. In fact, that perception was shared by Mme de Grignan, according to her mother: "Vous me dites que vous êtes fort aise que je sois persuadée de votre amitié, et que c'est un bonheur que vous n'avez pas eu quand nous avons été ensemble" (1:226). The preceding was written in 1671, and eight years later, a similar tone still prevails: "Je ne me souviens plus de tout ce qui m'avait paru des marques d'éloignement et d'indifférence; il me semble que cela ne vient point de vous, et je prends toutes vos tendresses, et dites et écrites, pour le véritable fond de votre coeur pour moi" (2:451). It is evident that those expressions of tenderness may have been more often written than said, and that Mme de Sévigné was more than willing to replace any signs of indifference or hostility—not uncommon during their periods together—with what was the preferred mark, although expressed in writing.

In a paradoxical way, then, absence allowed for a more satisfactory expression of love than did presence; and it can be said that writing did emerge as superior to being together, although on the conscious level the latter was the expressed, desired goal. But writing was heavily relied upon to communicate "true" feelings, those superior emotions free of any bitterness, which Mme de Sévigné judged to be the real mark of the relationship with her daughter. That she saw the possibility of achieving the perfection she had mentally established as inherent in her involvement with Mme de Grignan is evident in the unusual recourse to writing even when her daughter was in or nearby Paris. Expressing herself via the written word was a means of achieving both a certain liberty and self-constraint through the working over and the manipulation of terms.[18] And it is a rather remarkable piece of writing that the marquise offers to her child while Mme de Grignan was visiting her:

Il faut, ma chère bonne, que je me donne le plaisir de vous écrire, une fois pour toutes, comme je suis pour vous. Je n'ai pas l'esprit de vous le dire; je ne vous dis rien qu'avec timidité et de mauvaise grâce; tenez-vous donc à ceci. Je ne touche point au fond de la tendresse sensible et naturelle que j'ai pour vous; c'est un prodige. Je ne sais pas quel effet peut faire en vous l'opposition que vous dites qui est dans nos esprits; il faut qu'elle ne soit pas si grande dans nos sentiments, ou qu'il y ait quelque chose d'extraordinaire pour moi, puisqu'il est vrai que mon attachement pour vous n'en est pas moindre. Il semble que je veuille vaincre ces obstacles, et que cela augmente mon amitié plutôt que de la diminuer: enfin, jamais, ce me semble, on ne peut aimer plus parfaitement. (2:408)

The perfect expression of her sentiments, the harmony, calm, and tranquillity which filter into that expression, can be obtained only through a letter. In choosing to communicate via writing, Mme de Sévigné implicitly states that although the relationship may seem imperfect, especially to Mme de Grignan, in essence it is sublime. The rest is appearance, sham, misunderstanding, a failure to relate. If the communication can be made more satisfactory, so too can the relationship; hence, the recourse is to writing. "Mes lettres sont plus heureuses que moi-même; je m'explique mal de bouche, quand mon coeur est si touché" (2:400).

This problem of what is "more real" is paramount in the letters. There is an ambiguity between absence and presence, imagination and reality, that is difficult to resolve. Aware of the possibility of *défiguration*, Mme de Sévigné proceeded, nevertheless, to (re)construct an elaborate, complex relationship far more successfully on the written level than on the "living" one. At the center of the correspondence is the altering of time, space, and the entire system of relating. Mme de Sévigné stressed the satisfaction of the individual psyche as the preeminent element in the structuring of a life "project," and consequently was governed only by that which could conform to it. The organization of her mental world had to fit the emotional demands she imposed upon it. Moreover, her fantasizing, her reconstruction of the world around her through the use of the written word, was exactly the option of an Esprit, of a Saint-Evremond, or of a La Rochefoucauld, although her demands differed considerably from each of those writers. If we feel more keenly her attempt to transform the universe to certain needs, it is perhaps because her effort was so obviously an intimate one, painted as such, with no recourse to an anonymous *on*. The dream somehow seems more fragile, the attempt to rebuild more vulnerable, because she left herself so exposed.

If, however, the marquise's struggle resembles in structure those of other classical moralists, particularly in the firm belief in the power of the word, her desire to live through her love, and the incessant expression of it, was not at all consistent with the three prevailing "moralist" currents: Jansenism, Epicureanism, and *la mondanité*. The latter two were challenged by her refusal—conscious or subconscious—to be guided by desire for repose or social adaptability. The letters to Mme de Grignan are far too intense ever to be considered as part of the gallant code, and in her refusal to live a present-oriented life, uninvolved and *disponible*, she clearly violated the precepts of Saint-Evremond and the Epicureans. In both cases it was the overwhelming totality of her passion—one that left little room for anyone or anything else—that was in opposition to the current vogues.

Nor do either of the codes seem to have obviously affected her. This was definitely not the case, however, for Jansenism, which appears, at first, to have been the greatest obstacle to Mme de Sévigné's involvement with her daughter. Clearly, her love for her child could never be tolerated by the Jansenists, for whom terrestrial love was viewed as a direct rival to man's love of God. However, the marquise's intellectual battle with Jansenism can be seen as the socialized form of her own private guilt, and as the sole force—sufficiently structured and well developed—able to control what she undoubtedly saw as a violent, potentially self-destructive passion. Recourse to the Jansenist ideals was her only means of counterbalancing her obsession, and although its tenets could not destroy her feelings, at least she could use them as a moderating power.

Mme de Sévigné experienced a vague, nebulous guilt concerning her passion for her daughter, although it is impossible to describe the precise source of that feeling. She had grave concern over the emotional demands and sacrifices that the relationship had placed upon both Mme de Grignan and herself. There are allusions to her own anxieties over the nature of her love, for example, when she finds it necessary to clarify for Françoise-Marguerite (and perhaps for herself as well) that when she says "amour" she means "amour maternel" (2:677-78). In any case, whatever the exact cause of the guilt, which runs through the letters, its most satisfactory expression was in religious terms.

The marquise thus came to perceive that her sentiments for her daughter were a violation of God's law. Mme de Sévigné was fully aware that in loving, in adoring, her daughter as she did, she was going counter to the stern Jansenist principles and therefore was not truly surprised when Arnauld d'Andilly scolded her for "idolatry" toward her daughter, or when a priest refused her absolution and communion during Pentecost (1:276, 729). How deeply she was concerned over the reprimands is questionable, as is the entire question of her involvement with Jansenism. What can be said is that the rigorous, Jansenist code served as a slight braking force on what would otherwise have been a totally uncontrolled passion. That she felt guilty, as most critics view the situation, for violating the Jansenist principles is not certain; what seems far more probable, judging from certain tones in the letters, is that she experienced a rather strong sense of guilt, and that Jansenism was a sound philosophy for tempering, even only moderately, her obsessive passion.

[109]

But the long, emotional struggle with this braking force was not a very successful one. Aware that her feelings bordered on deification, Mme de Sévigné nevertheless failed to make use of the Jansenist tenets in any substantial way. Ultimately, she opted for idolatry and for the free expression of her emotions. By judging and conceding her failure in advance, by stating multifold times that she was too weak to oppose her passion, she thereby allowed for the liberty of living and expressing herself as passionately as she did: "Et quand nous sommes assez malheureux pour n'être point uniquement occupés à Dieu, pouvons-nous mieux faire que d'aimer et de vivre doucement parmi nos proches et ceux que nous aimons" (2:643). Jansenism was there to serve as a constant reminder to her of the extent of her involvement, to temper the tendencies toward uncontrol, but it was also prejudged unsuccessful.

The only substantial comfort she obtained from the precepts of Jansenism was through the idea of a Providence that she came to see as "willing" the separation of mother and daughter. But this too offered only a means to emotional equilibrium that she could not easily realize. An increasingly strong reliance upon submission to Providence can be detected over the span of twenty-five years, thus giving rise to a theory of religious conversion.[19] Nevertheless, it seems most accurate to conclude, as has Harriet Ray Allentuch, that the heavy dependence upon the ways of Providence was not only "a substitute for painful thoughts" but also a means to absolve both herself and especially Mme de Grignan of any responsibility. "If Madame de Sévigné conceived the suspicion that her daughter might not be doing her utmost to arrange the Grignans' permanent return to Paris, she need only push the phantasm aside."[20]

Too much time has been devoted, however, to the problem of Jansenism in Mme de Sévigné's life and letters. The strict tenets were primarily a means to self-control. The central problem of the correspondence still remains one of penetrating the nature of its origins and expression. A definite choice of structuring life was made, along grounds that were at once personal and general. The obsession with Mme de Grignan was individual, try as the marquise did to endow it with a sense of collective concern. But to base an entire adult life upon this passion, to write about it, to interpret it again and again, to explain, to justify, are needs whose limits are precisely and persistently intertwined in the double domains of love and language.

1. Gustave Lanson, *Choix de lettres du dix-septième siècle* (Paris: Hachette, 1913), p. 482.

2. Ibid., p. 483.

3. Roger Duchêne, *Réalité vécue et art épistolaire: Madame de Sévigné et la lettre d'amour* (Paris: Bordas, 1970), pp. 237-38.

4. Madame de Sévigné, *Lettres*, ed. Gérard-Gailly, 3 vols. (Paris: Bibliothèque de la Pléiade, 1953), 1:41. All subsequent references are to this edition, and will be found in the text. The richest and most informed edition of Mme de Sévigné's letters is undoubtedly the recent, but not yet completed, one by Roger Duchêne for Bibliothèque de la Pléiade. Unfortunately, only the first volume was available when I wrote this chapter.

5. Jean Cordelier, *Mme de Sévigné par elle-même* (Paris: Seuil, 1967), pp. 36, 79.

6. Bernard A. Bray, *L'Art de la lettre amoureuse* (The Hague: Mouton, 1967), p. 12 n. 18.

7. Cordelier, *Mme de Sévigné par elle-même*, p. 35.

8. As examples of the two poles of thought, Cordelier stresses the first interpretation, and Harriet Ray Allentuch, in *Madame de Sévigné: A Portrait in Letters* (Baltimore: Johns Hopkins University Press, 1963), accentuates the second.

9. Cordelier, *Mme de Sévigné par elle-même*, p. 33.

10. Eva Marcu, "Madame de Sévigné and Her Daughter," *Romanic Review* 51 (October 1960): 187.

11. Cordelier, *Mme de Sévigné par elle-même*, p. 33.

12. Duchêne, *Madame de Sévigné et la lettre d'amour*, p. 54.

13. Cordelier, *Mme de Sévigné par elle-même*, p. 80.

14. Allentuch, *Madame de Sévigné*, p. 40.

15. Ibid., pp. 40-41.

16. Ibid., p. 42.

17. Bernard Bray, "Quelques aspects du système épistolaire de Mme de Sévigné," *Revue d'histoire littéraire de la France* 69 (May-August 1969): 500-501.

18. Duchêne, *Madame de Sévigné et la lettre d'amour*, p. 172.

19. Ibid., p. 235.

20. Allentuch, *Madame de Sévigné*, pp. 201-2.

Chapter Six

# JACQUES ESPRIT

T NO MOMENT of French literary history has Jacques Esprit been favored with critical appreciation. Twentieth-century critics, if they mention at all his work *La Fausseté des vertus humaines*, usually dismiss the Jansenist writer as being too didactic and consequently of little interest to the modern reader. Even if this were the case, it would not explain why we read and study the works of other moralists whose tone is scarcely less didactic than that of Jacques Esprit. Among the seventeenth-century prose writers, Esprit has indeed been virtually ignored. But the reason lies perhaps not in his didactic style, so common to the time, but rather in the position his work occupies in relation to La Rochefoucauld's *Maximes*. The two writers were close friends over a long period of time, and unquestionably, a mutual influence exerted itself in their writings.[1]

The *Maximes* is surely the stylistically superior work. Its barbs, its stings, its highly structured, terse sentences overshadow the long-winded and frequently repetitious pronouncements on human behavior in *La Fausseté des vertus humaines*. Esprit's book, pontifical and heavily dosed with Jansenist doctrine, becomes a foil against which the critics can better measure La Rochefoucauld's finesse. When he is not tightly bound to the author of the *Maximes*, Esprit is grouped among several "moralistes jansénisants"[2] whose ideas are then studied collectively. Neither method does justice to Esprit's work.

My analysis of *La Fausseté des vertus humaines* is necessarily limited here to the ideas on human relationships, which form perhaps the most vital parts of the work, for terrestrial love constitutes the greatest threat to man's tie to his God. Before entering into that subject, however, it is necessary to situate more fully M. Esprit's work.

Published in 1677 and 1678, the two-volume work lashed out above all at devout humanism. The belief in man's "good nature" is systematically destroyed, as are all notions of the human creature rivaling God for ultimate worth. Man's "virtue" (understood to mean his generosity, his kindness, and all other humanistic elements forming the composite *homme vertueux*), is shown to be an unmitigated sham. Underneath the appearances, below the surface, there are hidden motives and concealed reasons that have always our own well-being at stake.[3] *L'amour-propre* is the leitmotiv of *La Fausseté des vertus humaines* and, for Esprit, the central pivot of all human behavior. Man is a monster of self-interest, and Esprit digs in hard, seizing every opportunity to rip off the mask of virtue.[4] In fact, the criticism that has long centered upon La Rochefoucauld's effort to strip man bare, to reach the irreducible unit of *l'amour-propre* (a theory questioned in my chapter on the author of the *Maximes*) is far more applicable to Esprit, for whom self-interest does constitute the one most fundamental element of human behavior.

What emerges is an attack against man's *volonté*, what Esprit sees as his wish for strong moral fiber, as well as his *bonne volonté*, which man believes generously leads him into relationships with his fellow men. Stoicism is laid to rest, as is the flexible Christian doctrine of the devout humanists, offering room for both man and God at its center. Esprit demands a constant stripping bare, a

[114]

persistent awareness that appearance and reality share nothing at all. His center of authenticity is always situated in *le coeur*, whereas modern-day psychology postulates a more complex and less regionally specific division (although generally mental) between act and motivation—the subconscious. Nevertheless, both reflect a constant trend in Western thought, the wish to somehow attain the "true" self. Indeed, it appears that Jacques Esprit expressed the entire concept of authenticity as fully as contemporary psychology, perhaps with less verbal acumen but with no greater degree of abstraction. Modern psychology and psychoanalysis have merely strengthened a culturally significant phenomenon, that of a functioning system independent of, and separate from, a center of conscious behavior. It has not yet explained or proved anything. The supposition of an unconscious remains hypothetical, although centuries of Western thought—through one vocabulary or another—have solidified it enough for us to schematize whole patterns of behavior.

But it would be erroneous to suggest that *La Fausseté des vertus humaines* is simply a psychic denuding, where fifty-three "virtues" are denounced as false for masking and hiding the one real motivating force in man, his self-interest. What also emerges from the work is a strict effort at controlling human behavior on all levels, from thought to act, through the word. It seems quite possible that at some junctures the severe Jansenist doctrine was in agreement with the prevailing social mood. Critics of the period have suggested that the general turbulence of the second half of the seventeenth century was a disturbing factor to large segments of the French population, and the sense of moral decay was eventually linked, unjustifiably or not, to the flexible complacence of the clergy.[5] The civil disorders had brought about a general awareness of society's fragile vulnerability, and the Jansenist tendency toward control, individual and social, matched the prevailing mood of restraint. For the Jansenist writers, what was needed were not the optimistic ideas that the church had readily espoused as a reconciliation between two totally distinct moral systems (the rivaling prerogatives of God and the self), but a rigorous separation of earthly and divine. In Jacques Esprit's work there is indeed no transition from one domain to the other.

He avoids a chapter directly on love, since Jansenism could not envision any terrestrial competition for adoration of God. Love, then, for Esprit, would not be considered a false virtue; it would simply be *hors du jeu*. But the truth is that Jacques Esprit does devote several pages to the subject in three different chapters of the second volume: "La Tempérance," "La Modestie des femmes," and "L'Honnêteté des femmes." The first discusses love within a rather general context of sentiment and emotion, whereas the latter two chapters focus specifically on *l'amour*. It is significant that Esprit is concerned with physical love in these chapters. He leaves Platonic relationships for the section on friendship.[6]

Writing on temperance, he pits himself directly against Aristotle, for whom desires were dangerous only if uncontrolled by a moderating spirit. For Esprit, however, desire, no matter how weak, is dangerous to man's psychic well-being. He decries most vehemently, however, the alienation that results from intensely experienced emotion. The individual who allows himself to be governed by the reign of passion denies that which is, for Esprit, most fundamentally human: reason. Within the context of the work, such a shift is basically a deviation from the psychic norm and is considered therefore as highly undesirable. Unable to control himself—unable, perhaps more importantly, to be controlled—man succumbing to the sway of violent feelings becomes not only asocial but inhuman. As protection against these psychologically and socially destructive impulses, the individual must combat them from incipience:

> [L'expérience] apprend à tout le monde que les passions sont séditieuses et déréglées en quelque état qu'on les considère: car si on les considère dans leur naissance, les

[116]

plus faibles de même que les plus violentes préviennent la raison, et n'attendent pas ses ordres pour s'élever. Or c'est un dérèglement manifeste, puisque c'est à la raison à donner le branle à toutes les puissances de l'âme, et que pas une ne doit se remuer que par sa direction; que si l'on examine ce qu'elles font dès qu'elles sont élevées, on voit qu'au lieu d'être souples et obéissantes à la raison, elles lui sont rebelles; qu'elles la combattent et qu'elles lui ôtent la liberté de juger, ou corrompent ses jugements. De plus, chaque passion après avoir aveuglé l'homme, l'asservit et l'attache à son propre objet.[7]

The servile state of man ruled by his emotions is rejected by Esprit, who seeks to install, or to reinstall, the reign of lucid reason. (Like Rousseau, a century later, he creates a myth-like fantasy of a golden time before man's essential corruption, an era, for Esprit, when man loved God alone, and the human creature was no rival.) Felicity is calm, sure, steady; and only a true Christian, one who abstains from sensual pleasure for love of God, not for a "false" reason such as avarice, can find such happiness.

His attack is a major thrust against the prerogatives of the self and the aristocratic code. As Paul Bénichou has written, noble society had never considered the censuring of passion, of the passions, as a condition of human worth. For the aristocracy, from the Middle Ages through the seventeenth century, "virtue" (grandeur of soul and spirit) was not in the denial of the passions but rather in their full expression. Medieval Christian moralists had found it necessary to denounce this "natural" moral, for it was in direct contradiction to the Bible's teachings.[8] In the seventeenth century a flexible form of Christianity, granting a high place to terrestrial love once freed from its grosser elements, combined with, or at least leaned upon, the *courtois* idea of love and its sublimated impulses, and thereby offered a successful compromise between a natural moral and a rigorously Christian one. For Jacques Esprit no such reconciliation is possible. His is a total rejection of nature's way, and sexual abstinence is requisite.

Although the chapter on temperance contains several pronouncements against the dangers of *la volupté*, Esprit's strongest attack and censure appear in two other chapters: "La Modestie des femmes," and "L'Honnêteté des femmes." In *La Fausseté des vertus humaines*, the burden and guilt of loving fall directly upon the woman, and Esprit's attitude contrasts sharply with the portrayal of women and love in the novels of the century, which were direct descendants of medieval *courtoisie*. The dependent position of women in seventeenth-century French society has been detailed by many critics and scholars, perhaps most thoroughly by Gustave Fagniez. It is not my intention here to repeat that position. But Esprit's ideas are unquestionably more in accordance with prevailing social standards for women than with the *romanesque* picture. Traditional ideas on woman's submissive role were strong, and as Molière expressed in *L'Ecole des femmes*, signs of revolt—fine clothing, makeup, flirtations—were vehemently condemned.

In both chapters Esprit is eager to explain the close attention he accords to women and their societal role. He clearly states that there are virtues appropriate to men and others that are the lot of women. Modesty is among the latter, for women have a "natural timidity" and coldness that are conducive to such caution (p. 91). The chapter on *l'honnêteté* begins with a bitter denunciation of woman's position in society, only to change quickly into a facile acceptance of the status quo:

> Mais peu de gens s'aperçoivent que l'amour propre a rendu tous les hommes de vrais tyrans, et que leur tyrannie, qui est cachée dans leur coeur, éclaterait par leurs cruautés si l'impuissance ne retenait leur férocité et leur violence. . . . Si quelqu'un trouve de la difficulté à croire qu'il soit généralement vrai que le naturel de l'homme est fier, farouche et inhumain; il n'a qu'à jeter les yeux sur tous les endroits du monde; il verra que les personnes riches et puissantes oppriment partout celles qui sont pauvres et sans appui; il verra que les hommes se prévalent partout des avantages que leur sexe leur donne sur celui des femmes;

qu'ils les traitent avec tyrannie, les font vivre sous des lois injustes et rigoureuses. . . . Ainsi le joug du mariage qui assujettit aux mêmes lois les femmes et les maris, n'asservit plus que les femmes; ainsi la chasteté qui doit être commune à l'un et à l'autre sexe, est devenue la vertu des femmes et des filles; et c'est ce qui m'oblige à la leur attribuer particulièrement, et à parler de l'honnêteté comme si c'était une vertu qui ne fût propre qu'à elles. (Pp. 100-102)

A bit too prompt to accede to the "way things are," Esprit's early criticism dissolves in face of his severe standards for judging women's conduct. Perhaps he felt self-exonerated after his profession of innocence. However, it is easy to penetrate beneath the surface protestation and glean a quick acceptance of the double standard. Since passion is woman's business, Esprit will offer her ways of protecting herself and, consequently, society against its demands.

It is against the tradition of *la courtoisie* and *l'amour honnête* that Esprit directs his anger. Seventeenth-century fiction writers are to be held responsible for the current vogue of sentimentality, for the depiction of love as a pure and generous sentiment: "Les Auteurs des Romans ont réussi dans l'entreprise qu'ils ont faite de persuader au monde que les femmes peuvent être galantes vertueusement et faire l'amour avec innocence . . . " (p. 105). For Esprit, this mixed moral of love and virtue is a radical impossibility, since the woman involved in a love relationship is "possessed." No longer governed by reason, subject to insensate anxiety, she is alienated from virtue. The marks of her soul are rage and jealousy: "Dire que l'amour est une passion honnête, c'est assurer qu'il est honnête d'être tourmenté par une furie, et de sentir tous les traits de la jalousie, de la rage et du désespoir" (p. 106).

Terrestrial passion, far from being innocent, is guilty of the most monumental of crimes: it detracts from divine love. There is no question for Esprit and the Jansenists of viewing love relationships, even chaste, as an imperfect form of divine love. Such affection is a rival, a serious threat to man's devotion to God; energy and time that might be used for religious worship are consumed in unworthy occupations directed toward the "other."

In "L'Honnêteté des femmes," Esprit returns to his leitmotiv of self-interest. Enumerating "false" motives for woman's wish to appear virtuous to the world, he methodically destroys whatever pride she may have in her conduct. Outside controls—a sound moral education, fear of punishment, desire to marry and remove herself from parental control—are not sufficient in Jacques Esprit's moral universe. He demands control from within, unmotivated by self-interest; and although his ideas at first reading sometimes appear banal, his thought, as it develops, frees itself from empty terms and becomes indeed a potent expression against immodesty.

Thus he first predictably states that "il n'y a que la modestie des femmes Chrétiennes qui soit une vertu véritable" (p. 98). Nevertheless, pushing further, he constructs an absolute standard for self-governance: "L'on peut . . . dire qu'une femme véritablement honnête ne doit pas seulement imposer silence aux vaines passions, mais aussi les étouffer dès leur naissance, et même les empêcher de naître" (p. 109). Esprit is now at antipodes from the more-or-less refined love of the *courtois* novel and from "le christianisme de sublimation" with its emphasis on adoration of saints and mystics. His vocabulary is one of total sexual repression—"imposer silence," "empêcher," "étouffer."

Nor does Esprit stop there. Not only must a woman (he never varies from the emphasis on female conduct after his lengthy self-exonerating introduction) appear so morally severe that no man dares approach her, she is also responsible for banishing all verbal expressions judged "impure" from her conversation: "Il faut encore qu'une femme véritablement honnête fasse comprendre . . . qu'elle n'entend pas le langage de ces passions, ni les signes qui font l'office de ce langage" (p. 110).

It is perhaps a result of the Cartesian revolution in the field of language that Esprit's work is so heavily impreg-

[120]

nated with allusion to the spoken and written word's enormous force. For him *la parole* is concomitant to *l'acte*, no less powerful or significant. Esprit clearly saw that the emotional charge of a word is as conducive to "immodest" desire as actions themselves. What he calls *des paroles sales* were invented by "les voluptueux . . . pour regoûter leurs sensualités par leurs entretiens, et pour allumer et irriter leur passion brutale" (p. 83).

Esprit delves even further. The stripping off of "layers" never reaches an end. There is always one more level underneath. Authenticity seems to be fleeting, at best. Unsatisfied with dissolving the layer of outer manifestation—first act, then word—Esprit comes to exact absolute control over the thought process, with God alone as judge. Following a semi-Platonic view, he states that thoughts, like words, are images of things, and therefore to be reckoned with as active, powerful forces. The secret language that is thought must be as free of longing and desire as the words and actions that interpret them.

Even with this, he has not reached the final "layer" of the self. "Below" the levels of action, word, thought, there is the motive for all these, and it too must be chaste, pure: "Il ne faut pas se contenter de savoir que leurs moeurs et leurs sentiments sont honnêtes; l'on doit encore tâcher de découvrir par quel motif elles gardent l'honnêteté, et établir auparavant quel est le motif qui la rend vertueuse" (pp. 115-16). In other words, there can be no distance between action, word, thought, and cause. No false motive must interpolate, and God alone shall judge: "Le coeur humain est un grand mystère. Les pensées et les désirs s'élèvent sur sa surface, et peuvent être aperçus. C'est pourquoi il n'y a personne qui ne sache ce qu'il pense et ce qu'il désire; mais les motifs des pensées et des désirs sont cachés dans sa profondeur, qui n'est pénétrée que des yeux de Dieu" (pp. 113-14).

What Jacques Esprit posits here, in his ultimate bow to divine wisdom, is essentially the same control modern psychoanalysis would see in the authoritative domination by the "superego," a construct no less questionable than "the eyes of God." In *Civilization and Its Discontents*, Freud, tackling the same problem as Esprit, that of the conflicting demands between the erotic and the social, hypothesizes a mental process akin to what Esprit had formulated in his work:

> The super-ego is an agency which has been inferred by us, and conscience is a function which we ascribe, among other functions, to that agency. This function consists in keeping a watch over the actions and intentions of the ego and judging them, in exercising a censorship. The sense of guilt, the harshness of the super-ego, is thus the same thing as the severity of the conscience. It is the perception which the ego has of being watched over in this way, the assessment of the tension between its own strivings and the demands of the super-ego.[9]

All this is not to suggest, of course, that Freud and his followers accorded the same moral supremacy, as if by right, to such "authority." They clearly saw the dangers for the individual in denying sexual fulfillment. What is significant is the similarity of the schematization drawn by seventeenth-century moralists and modern psychologists. The essential divisions of control and subordination, differing only in context (religious and "scientific"), remain the same.

There is at least one other important similarity between Esprit's ideas and the concepts of twentieth-century psychology and psychoanalysis. Both schemas seem to show that by stripping off the "layers," by probing "deep down," by peering beneath the surface to reach the hidden motives, we will eventually dispel them. Once a state of psychological transparency is achieved, the individual will return to a healthy state of mind, able to control impulses that may threaten his equanimity. Esprit's book is consequently a careful, explanatory work, showing the way to total self-knowledge, leading the reader step by step from action to motivation, toward ultimate personal frankness. Self-deception can be chipped away, and the individual can achieve heightened awareness, allowing him to govern his strong desires.

1. Antoine Adam, in the fourth volume of *Histoire de la littérature française au XVII<sup>e</sup> siècle*, 5 vols. (Paris: Donat, 1948–62), and more recently, Louis Hippeau in *Essai sur la morale de La Rochefoucauld* (Paris: A. G. Nizet, 1967), have shown the literary and philosophical debts Esprit and La Rochefoucauld owed each other. Hippeau, however, in stressing Esprit's allegiance to Jansenism, evokes the great gulf that ultimately divided the two writers. In *La Religion des Classiques* (Paris: Presses universitaires de France, 1948), Henri Busson accentuates the psychological rather than the religious bent of *La Fausseté des vertus humaines*, showing how close Esprit's ideas were to those of La Rochefoucauld.

2. Paul Bénichou, *Morales du grand siècle* (Paris: Gallimard, 1948), p. 161.

3. The vocabulary of "layers" is extremely important to Jacques Esprit's writings, as it is also to twentieth-century psychology. Perhaps it is the best conceptualization of authenticity, of "true self-ness" that can be offered. Of course, the *être-paraître* distinction runs rampant through seventeenth-century literature, especially after Corneille. Thus Esprit's constant use of "layered" vocabulary can be seen as a psychological fabrication, which stuck, and as a variation of a particular socio-literary theme.

4. As other critics have all carefully explained, the frontispiece of *La Fausseté des vertus humaines* shows the mask of virtue falling from Seneca's face, thereby leaving exposed the true visage of the philosopher. But the man who discovers it is shown averting his eyes, turning them toward another figure whose name is "Vérité" and who signifies the only true path, Christian virtue and grace. This goes one step further than the frontispiece of the *Maximes*, where Seneca's unmasked face *is* the ultimate truth: there is no Christian rival.

5. Henri Brémond, *Histoire littéraire du sentiment religieux en France*, vol. 1, *L'Humanisme dévot* (Paris: Bloud & Gay, 1916), pp. 388–89.

6. It is perhaps in the chapter on friendship that Esprit is more clearly inspired by his friend La Rochefoucauld. *L'amitié* is denounced as a false virtue, for self-interest alone prompts us to seek out the companionship of others. What is most interesting in the chapter is the analysis that Esprit offers of Montaigne's close, intense relationship with Etienne de la Boétie, one that Esprit perceives as bordering on feelings of love.

7. Jacques Esprit, *La Fausseté des vertus humaines*, 2 vols. (Paris, 1678), 2:25-27. Subsequent references are to this edition, and will be found in the text; all quotations are from volume two.

8. Paul Bénichou, *Morales du grand siècle*, pp. 21-22.

9. Sigmund Freud, *Civilization and Its Discontents*, ed. James Strachey (New York: W. W. Norton & Co., 1961), p. 83.

Chapter Seven

## THE *LETTRES PORTUGAISES*

UIS-JE OBLIGÉE de vous rendre un compte exact de tous mes divers mouvements?"[1] The letters of *la religieuse portugaise* are thus abruptly terminated, the final question a metacommentary on the entire project: a delineation of the multiple crosscurrents—conscious and subliminal—that filter through the nun's mind, reflecting her one obsession (the betrayal) in shifting, rotating perspectives. The silence that follows is complete; there is no intervening explanation, no addendum, no conclusion by a third party, no hints of the future at all. Unlike *Les Liaisons dangereuses* and *Adolphe*, both works that concentrate upon obsessive passion and authoritatively allude to the punishments of the diverse characters, thereby offering a moral stamp, the *Lettres portugaises* fall into an ambiguous silence, total, but as troublesome as the muteness that overtakes *Bérénice*, expressed in Antiochus' withered "hélas," silence without clarification, without conclusion, without poetic order. This ambiguity alone would seem to have demanded critical notice, and yet it is only recently, in the article of Leo Spitzer in 1953, that the *Lettres portugaises* have been explored beyond the preliminary level of authenticity and beyond an insidious effort to re-create the tale of the nun in a heavy, supinely *romanesque* fashion.[2]

The long debate over authenticity (Stendhal, Sainte-Beuve, Rilke, and various scholars convinced that the letters are indeed those of Mariane Alcaforado, "religieuse à Beja entre l'Estramadoure et l'Andalousie,"[3] thus substantiating the claim of the original publisher, Claude Barbin; Rousseau, Barbey d'Aureyvilly, and other critics sure that the letters are apocryphal) has been decided in favor of the latter group: Guilleragues, a seventeenth-century man of letters and friend to Racine, is now the accepted author.[4] A careful reading of Guilleragues' *Valentins* readily supports the case for his authorship of the *Lettres*, so frequently do certain basic themes recur. Literary history aside, however, the *Lettres portugaises* offer a complex web of psychological intrigue, layers of motivation and manipulation, and, above all, a decided pattern tracing the movement of a passion, inevitable in both its birth and death.

The work is short: five letters to the unfaithful French lover who has abandoned Portugal and his mistress to return to France. It is perhaps the brevity of these letters that inhibits the critical output, but their concision is precisely why they are of significance in a study of *l'amour-passion* in the classical age. More than any tragedy of Racine, they observe the demands of unity[5]—the walls of the convent restrict the boundaries of space, and although approximately one year is allowed to elapse, there is never really any sense of time passing, only a monotonous, stagnated repetition, an amassment rather than a continuous flow. Temporally, spatially, everything is limited, closing in upon itself.

The restriction of time and space corresponds perfectly to the reduction in action. Beyond Mariane's obsession there is nothing else: no decor to speak of, local flavor being almost totally excluded; no delineation of character, the French lover singularly colorless; no action exterior to the diverse movements, impulses of the passion itself. The reactions of the lover in the few brief lines he sends are never made truly clear—it is only his silence that is revealing. Mariane herself is interesting only in her monomania. What emerges from the complete absence of decoration, from this total nudity of situation, is a barren, harsh exposure of *l'amour-passion*, with the incessant monologue repeating its one theme of betrayal. Ultimately, there remains only the voice of the passion itself, Mariane's particular drama serving merely as the backdrop.

And yet the *Lettres portugaises* offer the portrait of one struggle not only against *l'amour-passion* but also against the entire myth of passion. The myth is that of Tristan and Isolde, and Guilleragues was in firm command of the legend. The close alliance between *l'amour* and *la mort*, an alliance that Mme de Lafayette did not fail to develop, is of prime importance in the *Lettres portugaises*, not merely as the private struggle of *la religieuse*, but also as literary convention that operates as a powerful controlling force within her emotional universe. Moreover, it is understandable that the seventeenth century would find in the Tristan myth a satisfactory expression of the problem of *l'amour-passion*. In Denis de Rougemont's *L'Amour et l'occident*, a case is made for the medieval formulation of the Tristan legend: "Le mythe, au sens strict du terme, se constitua au douzième siècle, c'est-à-dire dans une période où les élites faisaient un vaste effort de mise en ordre sociale et morale. Il s'agissait de 'contenir,' précisément, les poussées de l'instinct destructeur: car la religion, en l'attaquant, l'exaspérait."[6] The problem of *l'instinct destructeur* was strongly at issue in classical France. A revival of the Tristan legend as legend, that is, as literary convention, seems likely in an age caught up with the attempt at subduing, suppressing, unreason.

Passion, then, as a desired ideal, desired even for the suffering inherent in it, functions in the *Lettres portugaises* at once as a new, private force—Mariane's own particular conflict—and as a conventional one that may be even stronger—the entire socio-literary tradition of *l'amour-passion*. As in the Tristan legend, death comes to assume for Mariane the qualities of action and voluntarism that are most thoroughly contradicted by passion, by that which is endured, by that to which we are resigned. Thus she believes that a self-determined demise, a suicide, alone can restore the autonomy of the self. Mariane craves death, or at least attempts to crave it. Her letters are filled with allusions to her failing health, to her wish to "die of grief." And yet, in the end, she assumes a radically new stance, strives to throw off her illness and her passivity in favor of calming the irrationality that has dictated her every thought since the departure of the lover.

Mme de Lafayette, in *La Princesse de Clèves*, adhered firmly to the Tristan legend, allowing the heroine to die at the end, but virtually through her own volition; not as a passive agent, but rather as the determining force of her own destiny. Thus Death becomes the sole counterforce to Eros. The nun of the *Lettres portugaises*, however, chooses her purge not in a transcendent death but rather through the outlet of her mind, through what Spitzer has seen basically as a Cartesian breaking-down process.[7] In effect her deductions, her analysis (particularly strong in the fifth and final letter), her eventual acceptance of the nature of her obsession, all testify to a striving to curb the disturbing, irrational element of the psyche. At the end not only is her passion laid to rest, but along with it the entire Tristan legend of the *Liebestod*. Through the sorting-out process, Mariane achieves a new freedom, a way out of her own psychic disarray and, most importantly, a way out of the myths handed down by generations.

But although it is necessary to have established first the direction of the *Lettres portugaises*, to have shown that Mariane's struggle is at once private and collective, that she is battling not only her own passion but the convention of passion also, it is nevertheless essential to trace the letters from their beginning rather than to remain fixed on the end passages, important as they may be. There are two principal structures in the five letters, reflecting two different time sequences. (There is really a third time structure, also, that of the reader who is the "recipient" of the letters, and whose forced complicity and guilt in the entire affair are natural results of the letter format.)

There is first of all the interval of the year, or slightly more than that, between the lover's departure for France —a departure that Mariane readily criticizes for its lack of true explanation—and the fifth letter, the final one in the series, which both closes out the past and opens onto the future, in a constant juxtaposition of remorse and anticipation. Within this time span, traceable from one letter to the next and especially noticeable in a contrast between first and last letters, various transitions occur, what Mariane refers to as "divers mouvements," and which may be fully analyzed by *la religieuse*, or which, passing beyond the conscious level of the nun, may be grasped by the reader alone. The central passage, or movement, is from celebration of death to reflection upon life, a transition most obvious between the third and fifth letters, but apparent also in the first two letters through reference to fainting, a "temporary" death. As offshoots of this one underlying theme are diverse transitions signaling changes in the emotional state of *la religieuse portugaise*. Early submission and passivity give way, in the end, to overt anger and aggression; from a sense of "other-worldliness," of transcendence beyond the ordinary life condition, Mariane slowly achieves a new sense of community and reality; finally, the extraordinary emotional turmoil that colors the first four letters, in different shades and gradations, succumbs ultimately to a longing for tranquillity and repose.

The gradual reenactment of the relationship between Mariane and *le chevalier* constitutes the second basic structure of the *Lettres*. The progression of the "love story" itself is in direct opposition to the state of the present relationship. As the events fade into an increasingly more distant past, as the lover establishes his physical and emotional distance from Mariane, she in turn more vividly recreates the drama of their encounters, and her erotic souvenirs assume an increasingly sharper coloration. Thus their romance remains nebulous, vague in the early letters and gradually affects precision and force. Only slowly does the reader learn of the secret meetings in the convent, and only slowly is the erotic nature of Mariane's preliminary ties to her lover revealed. In a constant shifting of temporal structure, Mariane moves back and forth between the past—increasingly more fulfilling—and the present with its rapid diminishing of satisfaction.

It is properly the rapid interchange of these two movements that is, that creates, the passion. The keen remembrance of past desire, desire that was then gratified, provokes the sharp descent, repeated multifold times, into a present void of fulfillment. In his analysis of Racine, and particularly in the short section he devotes to the *Lettres portugaises* as they may have influenced that writer, Charles Mauron reminds that it is only impeded, obstructed love, love that is therefore not realizable, that engenders the "passion" situation. *L'amour-passion* focuses on objects that are at once absent and present, desired and forbidden. "Le désir bloqué se mue en angoisse, reflue, tourbillonne, se charge de persécution, de magie, de remords."[8] However, Mariane's passion will eventually wither from what Spitzer has called "inanition sentimentale," from lack of direct or indirect sustenance; and in the end she does achieve, or is at least on the way to achieving, a suppression of her feelings. A more detailed study of the five letters is now necessary in order to trace the nuances and modulations of Mariane's extraordinary preoccupation.

"Considère, mon amour, jusqu'à quel excès tu as manqué de prévoyance" (p. 39). Even as the more intimate *tu* quickly shifts to *vous*, the first letter remains familiar, cajoling, *précieux* in its tone. The flirtatious nature of this first communication will gradually give way to reproach, then to anger; but for now *la religieuse* is eager to establish what she perceives to be the reciprocity of sentiment. The unit of the couple is still strongly present in her mind, intact, and the movement toward emotional distance and separation, toward solitude, will come only in a slow, steady progression of awareness. For the time being, the Edenic situation is faithfully maintained: "Je suis résolue à vous adorer toute ma vie, et à ne voir jamais personne . . . " (p. 41). Thus Mariane successfully excludes the world, that is, her family and her religion.

However, it is particularly the *précieux-courtois* tone that dominates the first letter, in sentences filled with allusion to an animated, significant (in the original sense) universe: "J'envoie mille fois le jour mes soupirs vers vous, ils vous cherchent en tous lieux" (p. 39). The ruling image is the Ovidian eye, the eye where love lodges, and, in an extension of the theme, where grief too resides. The entire introductory section plays on the eye metaphor:

> Quoi! cette absence, à laquelle ma douleur, toute ingénieuse qu'elle est, ne peut donner un nom assez funeste, me privera donc pour toujours de regarder ces yeux dans lesquels je voyais tant d'amour, et qui me faisaient connaître des mouvements qui me comblaient de joie, qui me tenaient lieu de toutes choses, et qui enfin me suffisaient? Hélas! les miens sont privés de la seule lumière qui les animait, il ne leur reste que des larmes, et je ne les ai employés à aucun usage qu'à pleurer sans cesse.
> (P. 39)

Although the intense passion does communicate itself in this section, as in the entire letter (the sense of obstacle, of blockage, is already anticipated by Mariane), it is on a decidedly reduced level, and the nun's ties to her lover are revealed through metaphor-charged language. The whole letter, as Spitzer points out, is viewed as a caress[9]— "Adieu, je ne puis quitter ce papier, il tombera entre vos mains, je voudrais bien avoir le même bonheur"—and her suffering is still minimal enough to be expressed in terms of pleasure—"Adieu, aimez-moi toujours; et faites-moi souffrir encore plus de maux" (p. 42).

But the consistent use of *précieux* imagery points to more than mere optimism on Mariane's part. She emerges as dominated by the myth of *l'amour-passion*, by the myth of passion as a desired, sought-after ideal, superior to any other life choice. Guilleragues' careful choice of metaphor, his overly lyric tones bordering on the banal, testify not only to Mariane's naïveté but also to a sense of her control

[131]

by a potent code. Mariane is surely determined to love, determined by love, but it is as if determinism is here viewed as a seduction by powerful myths.

By the second letter, however, the coquettish tone has virtually disappeared, and Mariane's progression toward the crisis becomes increasingly stronger, charged now with bitterness and rancor. She has adopted the traditional posture of the female subjugated by the male, and her outcry is molded by this role of submission. It is not her pride that dictates her words, nor any sense of fear of punishment (this element is singularly absent from the work), but only her overwhelming preoccupation with the betrayal. The anguish is couched in metaphors of the woman-slave, and though the image ideally communicates the extreme limits of her depressive anxiety, it also echoes back to a long, literary tradition, (in the same way that later the allusion to a nun as the most perfect mistress, free from terrestrial preoccupations, will recall the medieval theme of the *clerc* as ideal lover):[10] "Ah! j'envie le bonheur d'Emmanuel et de Francisque; pourquoi ne suis-je pas incessamment avec vous, comme eux? je vous aurais suivi, et je vous aurais assurément servi de meilleur coeur: je ne souhaite rien en ce monde, que vous voir" (p. 45).

The persistent self-humiliation becomes increasingly more difficult to read, so much does *la religieuse* bow to the illusory perfections of her *chevalier*, her adoration bordering on idolatry, the cult of the lover replacing the one for God. Mariane herself announces a singular indifference for religion: "Je suis ravie d'avoir fait tout ce que j'ai fait pour vous contre toute sorte de bienséance; je ne mets plus mon honneur et ma religion qu'à vous aimer éperdument toute ma vie, puisque j'ai commencé à vous aimer" (p. 45). This chant, repeated in various fashion throughout the letters, becomes almost a litany of adoration, religious expression constantly intermingling with erotic, private desire. In an almost direct appropriation of Christ's words to his God, she exclaims at the end of the second letter: "M'avez-vous pour toujours abandonnée"

[132]

(p. 46)? Indeed, the entire theme of abandonment, situated in this sacred decor, seems to exist frequently on a level of sacrilege.

The second letter also marks the birth of two concepts subliminally perceived by Mariane, fundamental, however, to the work. It is now that the first substantial explanation of the relationship is offered, and the vocabulary and images, before molded by *la préciosité*, thereby reducing their power, now assume an obviously erotic base:

> Mes douleurs ne peuvent recevoir aucun soulagement, et le souvenir de mes plaisirs me comble de désespoir: Quoi! tous mes désirs seront donc inutiles, et je ne vous verrai jamais en ma chambre avec toute l'ardeur et tout l'emportement que vous me faisiez voir? mais hélas! je m'abuse, et je ne connais que trop que tous les mouvements qui occupaient ma tête et mon coeur n'étaient excités en vous que par quelques plaisirs, et qu'ils finissaient aussi tôt qu'eux; il fallait que dans ces moments trop heureux j'appelasse ma raison à mon secours pour modérer l'excès funeste de mes délices, et pour m'annoncer tout ce que je souffre présentement: mais je me donnais toute à vous, et je n'étais pas en état de penser à ce qui eût pu empoisonner ma joie, et m'empêcher de jouir pleinement des témoignages ardents de votre passion; je m'apercevais trop agréablement que j'étais avec vous pour penser que vous seriez un jour éloigné de moi. (P. 44)

As the distance separating the encounters grows, the memories become increasingly more vivid, Mariane experiences not only the diminishing of a reality found most satisfactory but, in reverse progression, a crystallizing of her emotional burn. Thus she (re-)creates her excitement through words, for they are all that subsist of the relationship, the sole elements that can, she believes, sustain her passion. The attempt at creation, at transforming her experience into "literature," is truly the only means open to Mariane for loving.

Finally, the second letter firmly establishes the limits of the role of the lover in the nun's world. The lack of a clear portrait, the scarce bit of information offered on him, was not by chance. Rather, if the person was depicted minimally, this decision translates the nature of Mariane's involvement: the Augustinian *amabam amare*. The letter's concluding section definitively closes out any other possibility: "Faites tout ce qu'il vous plaira, mon amour ne dépend plus de la manière dont vous me traiterez" (p. 46). Her passion reveals itself as functioning totally independently of the lover's reactions. It has now assumed a quality of complete autonomy, a trait that will prevail throughout the remaining letters. In the end, of course, Mariane's freedom is only from herself, from her rigid, self-created existence. Moreover, as the passion comes to function separately from the world of the lover, the concept of "writing" assumes an even greater role, and each letter becomes ever more difficult to close.

One sentence, in particular, serves to illustrate the general mood and tone of the third letter: "Je ne sais ni ce que je suis, ni ce que je fais, ni ce que je désire: je suis déchirée par mille mouvements contraires" (p. 48). Mariane has begun some critical questioning, and has at least broken ground in her appraisal of the situation. The movement toward "uncoupling" is fully in action as she separates herself from the lover, the increasing distance in space (as the *chevalier* continues his home voyage) corresponding to the distance she now perceives in their emotional states. But she is also questioning the nature of her own attachment. Although, in the final words of the letter, Mariane returns to the passive, submissive state that has long been holding sway, nevertheless there is a heightened awareness of her continued detachment from the person of her lover, if not yet from her passion itself. "Traitez-moi sévèrement! Ne trouvez point que mes sentiments soient assez violents! Soyez plus difficile à contenter! Mandez-moi que vous voulez que je meure d'amour pour vous. Et je vous conjure de me donner ce secours, afin que je surmonte la faiblesse de mon sexe, et que je finisse toutes mes irrésolutions par un véritable désespoir" (pp. 49-50). This strong demand that the lover now force Mariane to new heights of feeling translates her own confusion, as the nun slowly begins to see that she is freeing herself from the binds of the relationship.

Thus *la religieuse* now comes to perceive that the expression of her despair surpasses the feeling itself. At the same time, she feels urges toward life—"Je fais autant de choses pour conserver ma vie que pour la perdre" (p. 49) —that contradict what she believes would be an attitude more in keeping with the pose of the abandoned mistress. Convinced that she should seek death, as ordered by tradition, Mariane recognizes, nonetheless, that a part of her yearns toward life, that even her passion is one means of realizing an intense existence, and thus concludes: "Je déteste la tranquillité où j'ai vécu avant que je vous connusse" (p. 50). In the love affair with the French soldier, she had emerged from a nonexistence, symbolized rather obviously by the convent and which she is now reluctant to give up, only to return to solitude and sexual repression. Thus the letters take on great meaning for her, as the means not only to make the passion endure but also as the transition back to the emotional vacuum from which she was abruptly removed for a short time. But that transition is not yet wholly achieved, and for the present, the important reference to letter-writing itself—"Mon désespoir n'est donc que dans mes lettres"? (p. 49)—remains primarily an allusion to creation, to art, to a pleasure entirely divorced from the *chevalier* himself.

Writing is no longer only an outlet for Mariane, no longer that which interprets an inner state. Rather, it has assumed its own independent justification, has gone beyond that passion itself, in that it has prolonged what Mariane recognizes as the forced limits of her own feelings. Without writing there is nothing, and the inability to close the third letter (there are five *adieux* all followed by more words), translates her dilemma. The final sentence, paradoxically, is nothing less than an opening: "Ah! que j'ai de choses à vous dire" (p. 50).

Mariane's fourth letter, the longest of the series,

demonstrates her new understanding of the limits of love, and she now seems fully aware for the first time that a passion develops from obstacle, from refusal, from the partner's "no." In a sense this understanding legitimizes the *chevalier's* coldness and distance, for Mariane herself had too readily said "yes," although she twists further to claim that, knowing how vulnerable she was, he therefore never should have seduced her. The reproaches, however, fade as she allows herself to relive the entire first encounter and subsequent seduction, and clothes her description in the most *romanesque* terms, exciting herself again as she re-creates the day she first saw her lover executing some difficult maneuvers on his horse. As she pushes forth in her efforts to revive the past, she is by necessity thus forced into a deliberate exclusion of the present:

> Mais je suis sans cesse persécutée avec un extrême désagrément par la haine et par le dégoût que j'ai pour toutes choses; ma famille, mes amis et ce couvent me sont insupportables; tout ce que je suis obligée de voir, et tout ce qu'il faut que je fasse de toute nécessité, m'est odieux; je suis si jalouse de ma passion, qu'il me semble que toutes mes actions et que tous mes devoirs vous regardent. (P. 54)

It is, of course, not only the present time she is excluding but rather the entire network of societal pressures exhorting Mariane to quit her narcissistic universe. In the final lines of the above quote ("je suis si jalouse de ma passion"), the truly autonomous nature of her world assumes its full measure. The passion itself, and not the *chevalier* long since departed, is definitively recognized as the force behind the monomania. Each letter is a stimulus for the next, and re-creation of the past affair through writing replaces any other possible form of existence: "Pourrais-je survivre à ce qui m'occupe incessamment, pour mener une vie tranquille et languissante? Ce vide et cette insensibilité ne peuvent me convenir" (p. 54). This overwhelming preoccupation with her narcissistic passion leads her to admit that she cannot conclude, that she cannot stop writing, for each halt in the flow of words is a recognition of the emotional vacuum awaiting her, each end a descent back into the passion-free society that surrounds her. Hence, she concludes that "j'écris plus pour moi que pour vous" (p. 58).

From the start the fifth and final letter will be "different," announced so by *la religieuse* herself: "Je vous écris pour la dernière fois, et j'espère vous faire connaître, par la différence des termes et de la manière de cette lettre, que vous m'avez enfin persuadée que vous ne m'aimiez plus, et qu'ainsi je ne dois plus vous aimer" (p. 61). Although in part the general content of the last missive repeats several themes earlier established, notably that her involvement functions independently of its supposed source, the lover—"J'ai éprouvé que vous m'étiez moins cher que ma passion" (p. 62)—nevertheless, certain new tones aggressively assert themselves. The theme of vengeance appears for the first time, Mariane imagining the satisfaction derived from the possibility of delivering the *chevalier* into her parents' hands, or from that of taking, one day, a new lover. Significantly, for the first time, the Frenchman is dismissed by Mariane; but since his departure is an already established fact, the discharge can only be symbolic: "Je vous renverrai donc par la première voie tout ce qui me reste encore de vous" (p. 61). This sudden assertion of aggressiveness, this burst of anger, this attack on the lover, all are accompanied by increased lucidity on the part of the abandoned mistress. In particular, there is a deepened understanding of the precise nature of her obsession: "J'étais jeune, j'étais crédule, on m'avait enfermée dans ce couvent depuis mon enfance, je n'avais vu que des gens désagréables, je n'avais jamais entendu les louanges que vous me donniez incessamment" (p. 68).

Thus the fifth letter will be properly the means of rebellion, Mariane finally accepting, although almost against her will ("Que ne me laissiez-vous ma passion?"), the lover's abandonment. Henceforth, she will be guided by desire for life—the suicide idea is absent here—and it will be precisely the new lucidity and reasoning process that will allow for her liberation. All thoughts are now directed toward the cure, however arduous it may be. That the task will indeed be difficult, that Mariane's present resolutions cannot be definitively ascertained are perceptions present throughout the letter; there is a persistent vacillation between a desire for silence and one for continued words. Perceiving that her new movement toward liberation, and toward emotional solitude, toward a life without her passion, is still only nascent and hence fragile, *la religieuse* falls back readily into the temptations of the old pattern, into the unending monologue. "Je veux vous écrire une autre lettre, pour vous faire voir que je serai peut-être plus tranquille dans quelque temps" (pp. 67-68). But the final section of the letter concludes on a different note: "Mais je ne veux plus rien de vous, je suis une folle de redire les mêmes choses si souvent, il faut vous quitter et ne penser plus à vous, je crois même que je ne vous écrirai plus; suis-je obligée de vous rendre un compte exact de tous mes divers mouvements?" (p. 69).

Although the resolution is not yet firm, the seed is planted now for Mariane's freedom. However, the liberation that she seeks—a liberation that will paradoxically return her to the restraints of the convent—is less from the person of her lover than from the self-imposed shackles of her correspondence, from the solipsism that translated itself through the written monologue. By the end—indeed, from the beginning, but most evident in the concluding letter—all that remains are the words, and the final recognition is that even they have failed to maintain the force of the passion.

The direction that Mariane will now choose, although never directly stated, emerges clearly. She rejects any transcendence. Tristan and Isolde's *Liebestod*, Héloïse's movement toward spiritual purification, Mme de Clèves' descent into illness and death, are not the options of *la religieuse portugaise*. Rather, hers is a decision firmly grounded in the emotional and metaphysical framework of the seventeenth century.

[138]

In her strivings to achieve a new emotional freedom, one that will by necessity force her back into the convent and family, thus really liberating her only from herself, Mariane envisions precisely the goal of her efforts. She yearns now for repose, for tranquillity: "Je connais bien que je suis encore un peu trop occupée de mes reproches et de votre infidélité; mais souvenez-vous que je me suis promis un état plus paisible, et que j'y parviendrai" (pp. 68-69). Yearnings for emotional peace constitute one of the major currents of the classical moralist literature. The influence of Jansenism cannot be overlooked, although it is significant that the theme appears frequently in Saint-Evremond's works, a writer who at least consciously divorced himself from the heavier mood of the century. Descartes, Bossuet, Pascal, Méré, Mme de Lafayette, Saint-Evremond, all were caught up in a vast, sweeping trend toward emotional repose, toward strict effort at controlling irrationality, from Descartes' well-structured, compact beast-machine theory[11] to Saint-Evremond's gamesmanship. Thus Mariane's letters come also to reflect this fundamental problem, and by the end of her correspondence, the struggle between reason and irrationality is fully absorbed. In the *Lettres portugaises*, the aspiration toward control appears as a decided reaction against Mariane's sexual awakening, and in this context the role of the convent is primary.

It is not that the convent functions as a striking inhibition of a religious nature. Mariane readily assures the *chevalier* that her ties to her religion are limited, at least in comparison with the emotions that bind her to him. There is, moreover, no fear of divine wrath, of punishment. But this does not mean that the convent is without significance; rather, the overwhelming sense of enclosure inherent to the convent setting is the ideal metaphor for translating Mariane's dormant state prior to the encounter with the Frenchman. Her bitter cry in the first letter, an outburst that contrasts with the generally teasing tone— "que ne me laissiez-vous en repos dans mon cloître?" (p. 41)—states perfectly her condition before and after the love affair. The arrival of the French soldier was very much her Pandora's box. The convent is not omnipresent throughout the letters, but by the end its power has reemerged as a strong, controlling force, in the form of Mariane's sudden new remorse. Her passion is dying, on its way to being successfully cloistered, no longer a threat to Mariane nor to the society that envelops her.

It is as if Mariane and her obsession have been swallowed up, obliterated, by an imposing structure, given concrete form through the convent. But as has been previously shown, Mariane's battle is twofold: against the private obsession and also against the collective myth of *l'amour-passion*. The acts of destruction that occur in the final letter, or at least the menace of those acts—the urge to deliver the French soldier into her parents' hands, the desire to burn his letters and mementos, and the final, abrupt movement into silence—are impulses that counteract both Mariane's private anxiety and the legend of love. In swiftly moving, analytical language, *la religieuse* is extricated from the grips of her obsessive passion, and from the entire tradition of erotic love as a desired ideal. Her repression is thus total.

However, if Mariane's movements to free herself are tied in part to certain conventions, social and literary in nature, then it would appear that many themes of the *Lettres portugaises* would be decidedly conventional also. The limits of Mariane's anguish are defined by her referential system, a system dependent upon a constant juxtaposition of private depression with literary convention. She perceives her own entanglement in terms of a specific tradition, craving death, for example, not only as a release but as the correct form the battle must assume. This yearning, however, is persistently worn down by her concomitant struggle toward life, an existential choice that she correctly views as violating the code.

Guilleragues, it should be noted, is also the author of sixty-four *Valentins*, a literary adaptation of a game, as he explains in "Au Lecteur":

Il y a longtemps qu'on a inventé le jeu des Valentins; mais on les a faits depuis peu en vers: voici ceux qui me sont tombés entre les mains. Il faut, pour bien composer le jeu des Valentins, mettre le nom de trente hommes et celui de trente femmes, dans soixante morceaux de papier séparés, et copier séparément aussi les soixante madrigaux. Après avoir tiré séparément le nom d'un homme et celui d'une femme, on tire deux madrigaux, pour voir ce qu'ils disent l'un à l'autre. Si ce sont des choses tout à fait éloignées, ou tout à fait vraisemblables, les effets différents du hasard peuvent être quelquefois assez agréables, et j'espère que cette diversité d'épigrammes sur toute sorte de sujet te divertira.[12]

The intention is clear; at stake is a game—by necessity structured, with predetermined rules—whose strategy demands easy recognizability. Convention is at a premium, for it is absolutely necessary that familiarity and generality submerge the particular. Curiously enough, in the thirty-two pieces directed to men by women, the basic themes of the *Lettres portugaises* are readily duplicated. Abandonment is the background for both works, but even in their detail the two correspond. Thus Mariane's early, *précieux* desire to be duped finds a corollary in the *Valentins*: "Vous voulez rompre notre affaire. / Hélas, cet aveu sincère / M'accable de désespoir; / Trompez-moi, je vous en conjur, / Et continuez de me voir: / Du moins abusez-moi, parjure" (p. 101).

In a similar fashion Guilleragues writes his epigrams to point to disillusionment, to fatality, to weak excuses for departures, to anxiety over a lover's lies. And Mariane's final resolution toward self-control is mirrored in yet another piece: "Puisque je ne suis plus aimable, / Il faut tâcher de n'aimer plus aussi" (p. 110). Thus tradition-laden themes of betrayal, of female masochism, of beguilement, of fate, and of death, all enter into an "original" work such as the *Lettres portugaises* and into a heavily contrived one like the *Valentins*. The easy conclusion would be that Guilleragues was simply limited in his expression, that he could barely move from "play" into something more "serious." But his use of convention in the letters is not in order to define, to explain, Mariane's upset state; rather, it functions as the expression that *la religieuse* herself adopts in her struggle. Tied in by her own set of reactions to the betrayal situation, she is also bound by the tradition of writing her feelings, of translating passion into literature. Seeking to conform, she naturally has recourse to conventional language.

Yet her efforts are truly in vain, and the results fall far short of the expectations. Mariane's is a double failure, for she is a double victim, one who is successfully manipulated by the *chevalier*, but also by myth-making. In the end she is definitively abandoned, unable even to deceive herself. Moreover, her one creation, the letters, have failed her as well, for they are able neither to sustain her passion nor to translate it into original art, freed from convention and capable of generating a heightened existence. That is why there is no ultimate transcendent death, no transcendence of any sort, but only the lucid acceptance of her solitude; and that is why the ending is not a conclusion, but only a rupture, a breaking off into silence. It is a termination that corresponds, curiously enough, to that of Racine's *Bérénice*, a tragedy based precisely on an inability to say *adieu* (Antiochus and Titus both experience this difficulty). The word itself, just as in the *Lettres portugaises*, assumes an ironic importance, for closure of any sort is impossible. When finally Bérénice assumes control and utters her *adieu*, it is the entire tragedy that is accompanying her into the Orient, into silence. There can be no true "conclusion," nothing but a cessation, and the rupture-end is as necessary to Guilleragues' work as to Racine's. Tragedy and letters are thus banished. There is no other way out, except to stop writing; otherwise, the play continues, and so do the letters. A cutoff must occur, and does.

It is thus not only to her passion that Mariane is bidding *adieu* (significantly, when the rupture does occur at the end of the fifth letter, there is no pronouncing the word, for it was in itself too literary a stance for Mariane; her release had to be achieved by different means) but to art, for it has proved an unsatisfactory alternative, not able to sustain her passion or to subsist on its own without turning in a labyrinth of convention. Early in the letters, Mariane perceived that her death, a suicide, would be ultimately more authentic than her words—"mon désespoir n'est donc que dans mes lettres?" (p. 49)—that there was something not genuine in this creation. But thoughts of death revealed themselves, too, as strictly conventional, and Mariane's final decision, to stop writing, is truly the only authentic one. Silence alone can halt the cycle.

1. Guilleragues, *Lettres portugaises*, ed. F. Deloffre and J. Rougeot (Paris: Garnier Frères, 1962), p. 69. All subsequent references are to this edition, and will be found in the text.

2. Claude Aveline, *Et tout le reste n'est rien* (Paris: Mercure de France, 1951).

3. F. C. Green, "Who Was the Author of the 'Lettres portugaises'?", *Modern Language Review* 21 (1926): 160. Green is citing a note in the *Journal de l'Empire* contributed by Boissonade, a bibliographer.

4. Introduction, *Lettres portugaises*, passim.

5. Leo Spitzer, "Les 'Lettres portugaises'," *Romanische Forschungen* 65 (1953): 96.

6. Denis de Rougemont, *L'Amour et l'occident* (Paris: 10/18, 1962; original edition, Plon, 1939), pp. 17-18.

7. Spitzer, "Les 'Lettres portugaises'," pp. 126-27.

8. Charles Mauron, *L'Inconscient dans l'oeuvre et la vie de Racine* (Aix-en-Provence: Publication des Annales de la Faculté des Lettres, 1957), p. 260.

9. Spitzer, "Les 'Lettres portugaises'," p. 114.

10. Ibid., p. 115.

11. Erica Harth, "Exorcising the Beast: Attempts at Rationality in French Classicism," *PMLA* 88 (January 1973): 19-24.

12. Guilleragues, *Valentins*, ed. F. Deloffre and J. Rougeot (Paris: Garnier Frères, 1962), p. 81. Subsequent references are to this edition, and will be found in the text.

Chapter Eight

## LA BRUYÈRE

HE FIRST EDITION of the *Caractères* appeared in 1688. Seven editions followed, the final one in 1694. By date La Bruyère does not belong to the group of writers under consideration here, whose works were published during the 1660s and 1670s. By tradition, however, he does. More often than not, the author of the *Caractères* is included in studies devoted to the classical moralists. Such critical flexibility may be explained by the work's fragmented form, akin to the *Pensées* and the *Maximes*, or by La Bruyère's extensive use of the character portrait, a literary phenomenon dating back to 1650 and to Mlle de Scudéry's *Grand Cyrus*. In short, the *Caractères* are viewed as the culmination of a long-standing social and literary trend, as "a *summa* of seventeenth-century portraiture, the end-term of a society's effort to portray, take stock of, and give meaning to itself."[1]

There are major differences, however, between the *Caractères* and the works of the moralists studied in this group of essays. Yet, it is only recently that La Bruyère has begun to receive his due as a decidedly un-classical writer. In particular, two studies by Jules Brody have emphasized aspects of La Bruyère's book that differentiate it from the works of his predecessors. Brody concentrates on La Bruyère's portrayal of a morally and spiritually empty generation, dedicated to money and social promotion, whose vapid lives the writer captured by a new and extensive use of a vocabulary that stressed the physical, material world: "Si La Bruyère s'obstinait à peindre ses contemporains par le dehors, c'est tout simplement parce que ses contemporains, surtout nobles, ne lui montraient plus autre chose."[2] In support of this view, Brody cites the following passage:

> La cour n'est jamais dénuée d'un certain nombre de gens en qui l'usage du monde, la politesse ou la fortune tiennent lieu d'esprit, et suppléent au mérite. Ils savent entrer et sortir; ils se tirent de la conversation en ne s'y mêlant point; ils plaisent à force de se taire, et se rendent importants par un silence longtemps soutenu, ou tout au plus par quelques monosyllabes; ils payent de mines, d'une inflexion de voix, d'un geste et d'un sourire: ils n'ont pas, si je l'ose dire, deux pouces de profondeur; si vous les enfoncez, vous rencontrez le tuf. ("Cour," 83)[3]

From this perspective the *Caractères* portray a superficial society, one without moral values, where life has become a routine of purposeless, mechanical repetitions, exemplified best by the courtier, whose movements are never progressive, only repetitive: "Il fera demain ce qu'il fait aujourd'hui et ce qu'il fit hier" ("Ville," 12).[4]

The mood of the *Caractères* is thus quite different from the works of La Bruyère's predecessors who feared not monotony but emotional chaos, not an empty spirit but an overburdened one. Strongly evident in their works is belief in control of the self, an idea that is most sharply defined perhaps by writers such as Saint-Evremond and Jacques Esprit, but obvious also, for example, in the letters of Mme de Sévigné, who sought to reorder the imperfections of the "raw" relationship through the medium of the written word.

For many of the writers studied here, emotional repose

is one solution to what they viewed as an upsetting moral climate. Recognizing the limits of Logos in a psychological universe governed by Eros, Mme de Clèves' retreat to the convent is a radical denial of the life forces. Silence and death become her sole means to freedom. Similarly, the *Lettres portugaises*, though offering the hope of a regained will, nonetheless depict a renouncement that spiritually leads nowhere. Mariane will return only to the embryonic existence she led prior to her encounter with the *chevalier*. Her victory is Pyrrhic: though she liberates herself from the binds of an unreciprocated love, Mariane is only "free" to return to the shackles imposed by convent life. The "win" over passion is a "loss" of vitality, a retreat into dormancy. But this inert existence, not unlike that of the princesse de Clèves, and perhaps only an intensified form of ataraxia is ultimately seen by Mariane as a desirable alternative to the turmoil of love.

The moralists grouped in this study, seeking to perfect an "outer self" capable of controlling erotic energy, established a distance between the emotive and the rational parts of the personality. To give in to the disorganizing life of passion meant renouncing psychological and social equilibrium. The age's hero, not surprisingly, was *l'honnête homme*, the incarnation of the controlled, aesthetic ideal. There is an urgency in these writers' works to reform the raw stuff of emotion, to harmonize the individual with the social, to tranquilize both. In this context alienation implies a loss of reason and control to the unconscious, spontaneous force of love.

Alienation is also, of course, a theme in the *Caractères*. Loss of reason is still implied, for the machine-like existence of the "characters" is totally antithetical to rational, reflective behavior. But the threat is different from the one perceived by the preceding generation, originating not in love but in the mindless pursuit of money and social status. The problem is no longer one of attempting to control the disorganizing but energy-charged love force. Instead, the *Caractères* portray a silly, petty, often grotesque universe where if emotions (other than financial gain and social climbing) have been checked, the resulting society is no better off for it. Love *per se* is not a problem for La Bruyère, who did not fear the violent eruption of spontaneous emotion. Rather, the society he saw about him had become so depersonalized, its members so superficial, that the passions could pose relatively little threat. They are dismantled in the *Caractères*, but not through a *morale* devoted to control. Indeed, they seem merely to fade in a non-committed society of moral lightweights, where love is yet one more superficial emotion confirming man's and society's mediocrity.

La Bruyère's pronouncements on love appear in two contiguous chapters, "Des Femmes" and "Du Coeur." Although neither chapter deals exclusively with the problem, love is at least the underlying force of the section on women; it is only one among many emotions described in "Du Coeur." (The seventeenth-century connotation of "heart" was highly inclusive, suggesting all non-reflective, spontaneous reactions.) "Des Femmes" is far more acerbic than "Du Coeur," and at least superficially is reminiscent of the close alliance Jacques Esprit established between the burden of love and womankind. One of the few critics to discuss in detail La Bruyère's views on love, René Jasinski, has detected a Christian stance in the *Caractères*, whereby the moralist comes close to portraying woman as a creature of perdition. If "Du Coeur" is more subdued, believes Jasinski, it is because the element of female irrationality is absent.[5] Although this distinction is valid, Jasinski fails to stress the component of grotesque absurdity in La Bruyère's portraits of female behavior, which separates the *Caractères* from the rigorous mood of Esprit's *La Fausseté des vertus humaines*. Nevertheless, "Des Femmes" offers a more bitter portrayal of love than "Du Coeur," which is, as Jasinski has correctly perceived, a basically male-oriented chapter.

Woven through both chapters are themes dear to the French moralists of the preceding decades. As in the writings of Pascal and La Rochefoucauld, love is pitted against ambition: "Les hommes commencent par l'amour, finissent par l'ambition, et ne se trouvent souvent dans une assiette plus tranquille que lorsqu'ils meurent" ("Coeur," 76). In the *Caractères* ambition is generally believed to last longer than love, and, in fact, is often one of life's constants: "Le cas n'arrive guère où l'on puisse dire: 'J'étais ambitieux'; ou on ne l'est point, ou on l'est toujours; mais le temps vient où l'on avoue que l'on a aimé" ("Coeur," 75). This follows closely both La Rochefoucauld—"On passe souvent de l'amour à l'ambition, mais on ne revient guère de l'ambition à l'amour" (*Max.* 490)—and Pascal, in the *Discours sur les passions de l'amour*—"Qu'une vie est heureuse quand elle commence par l'amour et qu'elle finit par l'ambition! Si j'avais à en choisir une, je prendrais celle-là. Tant que l'on a du feu, l'on est aimable; mais ce feu s'éteint, il se perd. Alors, que la place est belle et grande pour l'ambition!"[6]

"Des Femmes," however, brings a new dimension to the love-ambition dichotomy. In "Du Coeur" La Bruyère views the problem with a good deal of resignation, establishing an equilibrium between two passions that, although they are the cause of substantial unease, are not truly destructive. The tone is quite different in the chapter on women, where female ambition is explicitly portrayed as troublesome: "Il est étonnant de voir dans le coeur de certaines femmes quelque chose de plus vif et de plus fort que l'amour pour les hommes, je veux dire l'ambition et le jeu: de telles femmes rendent les hommes chastes; elles n'ont de leur sexe que les habits" ("Femmes," 52). In the catalogue of female horrors compiled by Bruyère, there is a passion still more disquieting (for the male) than love: ambition. Significantly, however, the latter is a socially related emotion. What the moralist appears to fear most is not love's upsetting spontaneity but rather the adoption by the female of male-type, specifically social, behavior. The alienating power of love diminishes here, as estrangement from the self is characterized as closely related to societal standards.

La Bruyère is perhaps most conventional in his praise of friendship. Not surprisingly, in "Des Femmes," the love-friendship division is posed in terms of male-female characteristics: "Les femmes vont plus loin en amour que la plupart des hommes; mais les hommes l'emportent sur elles en amitié" ("Femmes," 55). When friendship is described in "Du Coeur," it figures as a rare but highly prized quality, much as in the writings of La Rochefoucauld and Saint-Evremond. Pure friendship is harder to achieve than love—"Il est plus ordinaire de voir un amour extrême qu'une parfaite amitié" ("Coeur," 6)—and the two passions are mutually exclusive—"L'amour et l'amitié s'excluent l'un l'autre" ("Coeur," 7). There is little new here, and La Bruyère seems to be making a concerted effort to be faithful to classical ideas and ideals.

On the other hand, La Bruyère's deference to the tradition of praising simplicity and naturalness engenders new thinking. The early parts of "Des Femmes" concentrate on the value of simplicity in women, with La Bruyère rejecting artificiality of all types. This theme had been particularly well developed by the chevalier de Méré, with whom the author of the *Caractères* is in ready agreement:

> Il y a dans quelques femmes une grandeur artificielle, attachée au mouvement des yeux, à un air de tête, aux façons de marcher, et qui ne va pas plus loin; un esprit éblouissant qui impose, et que l'on n'estime que parce qu'il n'est pas approfondi. Il y a dans quelques autres une grandeur simple, naturelle, indépendante du geste et de la démarche, qui a sa source dans le coeur, et qui est comme une suite de leur haute naissance; un mérite paisible, mais solide, accompagné de mille vertus qu'elles ne peuvent couvrir de toute leur modestie, qui échappent, et qui se montrent à ceux qui ont des yeux. ("Femmes," 2)

The intensity of La Bruyère's criticism, however, distinguishes his views from similar ones in other moralists' works. Women who use too much makeup not only fail to please; they are horrible—"Je leur prononce, de la part de tous les hommes ou de la plus grande partie, que le blanc et le rouge les rend affreuses et dégoûtantes; que le rouge seul les vieillit

et les déguise; qu'ils haïssent autant à les voir avec de la
céruse sur le visage, qu'avec de fausses dents en la bouche,
et des boules de cire dans les mâchoires" ("Femmes," 6).
Older women, La Bruyère writes in the following reflection,
are "disfigured" by such attentions. Thus females who fail
to conform to certain standards of beauty are grotesque and
distorted. If La Bruyère is repulsed by such women, as
Jasinski believes, his tone reflects, nevertheless, a well-
tempered horror. He sees the situation as nonsensical and
irrational, but also as comical. His descriptions provoke a
feeling similar to that produced by carnival distorting mir-
rors. One is simultaneously horrified and amused by the grotesque images they produce.

This tone dominates much of what La Bruyère has to say
on women and love. Both "Des Femmes" and "Du Coeur,"
for example, stress that love is an involuntary force, spontaneously erupting with no forewarning: "L'amour naît
brusquement, sans autre réflexion, par tempérament ou par
faiblesse: un trait de beauté nous fixe, nous détermine"
("Coeur," 3). Highly reminiscent of Mme de Lafayette's unvarying emphasis on the spontaneous immediacy of love,
La Bruyère's maxims and reflections are equally unvarying
in their diagnosis of an uncontrolled and uncontrollable force.
But there is, as usual, a qualitative difference between the two
chapters. What in "Coeur," 3, is a generalized statement,
faithful to the classical tradition, becomes in "Des Femmes"
an exposition of women's highly bizarre inclinations in love
matters: "A juger de cette femme par sa beauté, sa jeunesse,
sa fierté et ses dédains, il n'y a personne qui doute que ce ne
soit un héros qui doive un jour la charmer. Son choix est
fait: c'est un petit monstre qui manque d'esprit" ("Femmes,"
27). The rapidity and the totality of the woman's decision,
translated stylistically by the very brief "Son choix est fait,"
heightens its incomprehensibility. This quality of troublesome, inexplicable (at least to the male moralist) behavior
adds to a general sense of female irrationality. In "Du
Coeur" "un trait de beauté nous fixe, nous détermine"; in
the chapter on women, the determining trait is more often

the grotesque or the bizarre: "Est-ce en vue du secret, ou par un goût hypocondre, que cette femme aime un valet, cette autre un moine, et Dorinne son médecin?" ("Femmes," 32).

The association of the female with irrational behavior was hardly a new theme for the era. Jacques Esprit, for one, placed the burden and guilt of loving directly on woman; but despite this strong bias in *La Fausseté des vertus humaines*, he allowed her some dignity by offering a means of salvation: rigorous self-control. There is very little dignity in "Des Femmes," no hope that the language of reason and self-control can tame the unpredictability of female behavior. For La Bruyère women's nature is hopelessly unreasoning, but this irrationality primarily takes the form of the grotesque and the absurd.

The consequences of such a shift are radical. Reading through "Des Femmes" and "Du Coeur," one may detect an implicit, but very strong, psychological freedom on the moralist's part. Although it is true that women are painted as irrational and seductive creatures, the portraits' tone reduces the menace considerably. Dorinne, who loves her doctor; Lélie, who worships only actors, musicians, and dancers; and Lise, who cannot stop making up; all are very silly, unreasonable women. Their absurdities, however, are individualistic and idiosyncratic. Such portraiture sharply distinguishes La Bruyère from his predecessors, who exposed what they perceived as the typical, universal dangers of *l'amour-passion*. In this shift from the universal to the individually idiosyncratic, love is not seen as an alienating force in itself. The potential for disruption does exist, of course, in individual whim and caprice that threaten to dismantle stable, traditional social values. But even these whims are portrayed as more ludicrous than fearsome. Many females are real "characters," to be sure, but nothing worse than that. Women may, moreover, be controlled by their *confesseurs* and *directeurs* (fools though they may be); but this dependent method of regulation would not have been acceptable to Jacques Esprit, Mme de Lafayette, or *la religieuse portugaise*, who demanded inner, self-directed guidance.

The *Caractères*, then, convey a sense of diminished danger. This mood may be achieved by what appears to be a deliberate reconstruction of a classical motif. Adopting a theme that had preoccupied La Rochefoucauld, the author of the *Caractères* refers extensively to the end of love. Thus in "Du Coeur," the third reflection, which refers to love's beginning—"L'amour naît brusquement"—is followed immediately by one alluding to its end—"Le temps, qui fortifie les amitiés, affaiblit l'amour ("Coeur," 4). There is no transition here; the period between beginning and end is ignored or curtailed, thereby creating an impression of love's rapid disintegration. The moment of love always seems to have passed in the *Caractères*:

> Ceux qui s'aiment d'abord avec la plus violente passion contribuent bientôt chacun de leur part à s'aimer moins, et ensuite à ne s'aimer plus. Qui, d'un homme ou d'une femme, met davantage du sien dans cette rupture, il n'est pas aisé de le décider. Les femmes accusent les hommes d'être volages, et les hommes disent qu'elles sont légères. ("Coeur," 17)

Love dies quickly, and even memories fade—"Les amours meurent par le dégoût, et l'oubli les enterre" ("Coeur," 32) —for the emotions are inherently limited—"Cesser d'aimer, preuve sensible que l'homme est borné, et que le coeur a ses limites" ("Coeur," 34). "Coeur," 17, is similar in theme to one of La Rochefoucauld's *maximes supprimées*: "Comme on n'est jamais en liberté d'aimer, ou de cesser d'aimer, l'amant ne peut se plaindre avec justice de l'inconstance de sa maîtresse, ni elle de la légèreté de son amant" (62). Both the *Maximes* (particularly the *Maximes supprimées*) and the *Caractères* establish the limits of the will in matters of love; both allude often to love's inconstancy. And both rely extensively on a vocabulary of sickness to portray the body's total involvement in *l'amour-passion*. This metaphor, however, changes drastically with La Bruyère.

In both *De l'amour et de la mer* and *De l'amour et de la vie*, La Rochefoucauld seeks to convey the diverse transitions of the love cycle, from the early joys to the final, stagnant depression. In the *Maximes* he proceeds likewise, although the emphasis on the initial stages of love is less prominent. Most of the adages stress the stale end of love, its terminal moments. But whereas La Rochefoucauld chooses to focus on the theme of a decaying, warped spirit, La Bruyère centers immediately on the possibility of healing. If the emphasis in the *Caractères* is on love as sickness, the predominant word is still *guérir*.

The healing process is a ready balm for all suffering: "On guérit comme on se console: on n'a pas dans le coeur de quoi toujours pleurer et toujours aimer" ("Coeur," 34). Even in "Des Femmes," where female irrationality and whim offer the greatest threat of disorienting man, if not of destroying him, recuperation is ever present:

> Le caprice est dans les femmes tout proche de la beauté, pour être son contre-poison, et afin qu'elle nuise moins aux hommes, qui n'en guériraient pas sans remède. ("Femmes," 15)

> Les femmes s'attachent aux hommes par les faveurs qu'elles leur accordent: les hommes guérissent par ces mêmes faveurs. ("Femmes," 16)

> On tire ce bien de la perfidie des femmes, qu'elle guérit de la jalousie. ("Femmes," 25)

In the *Maximes*, however, healing is viewed as a far less reliable force:

> Il y a des rechutes dans les maladies de l'âme, comme dans celles du corps. Ce que nous prenons pour notre guérison n'est le plus souvent qu'un relâche ou un changement de mal. (*Max.* 193)

> Il y a plusieurs remèdes qui guérissent de l'amour, mais il n'y en a point d'infaillibles. (*Max.* 459)

Where La Rochefoucauld evinces only skepticism toward emotional healing, La Bruyère quickly ushers in total restoration to good health. However, there is in the *Caractères* a decidedly negative side to this salubrity. The "characters" may be quickly restored since, in terms of the depth of their love, they have never been very "sick." They heal quickly, it is true, but perhaps only because of their moral transience.

Inconstancy (fickleness is probably a more appropriate term) is one form of living adopted by this morally mobile society. Short-lived *galanteries* abound in the *Caractères*. Rarely is there a mutually deep exchange; one partner is always playing, play-acting, genuinely free of emotional involvement, and this freedom is achieved without the struggle waged, for example, by Mme de Lafayette's heroines or by *la religieuse portugaise*:

> Il coûte peu aux femmes de dire ce qu'elles ne sentent point: il coûte encore moins aux hommes de dire ce qu'ils sentent. ("Femmes," 66)

> Il arrive quelquefois qu'une femme cache à un homme toute la passion qu'elle sent pour lui, pendant que de son côté il feint pour elle toute celle qu'il ne sent pas. ("Femmes," 67)

In a portrait where the elusive style reflects perfectly the story's moral, secretive Glycère feigns faithfulness to her credulous husband, all the while indulging in a quantity of illicit relationships. From passages such as these, there emerges a mood of sham and emptiness. Feeling is so inconsequential that risk is always minimal. Inversely, as the superficial relationships indicate, there is never great depth of feeling. "Aussi bien," concludes Jasinski, "l'expérience prouve-t-elle qu'il [l'amour] donne lieu à des entraînements violents mais souvent sans profondeur vraie, que dans l'immense majorité des cas il s'engoue de façon déconcertante, multiplie les inconséquences et se perd dans la légèreté. La passion de toutes la plus puissante, celle par laquelle s'éprouvent le mieux les caractères, confirme la médiocrité de l'homme."[7]

In fact, the mediocrity of love is the basic theme of the two chapters. If there is no longer a need to harmonize, to tranquilize, the emotions, it is because depth of feeling, and hence emotional risk, is forceably excluded in a switching and swapping society: "Un ancien galant tient à si peu de chose, qu'il cède à un nouveau mari; et celui-ci dure si peu, qu'un nouveau galant qui survient lui rend le change" ("Femmes," 19). What has destroyed the society of the *Caractères* is not love, not the suffering and disorientation associated with it, but rather a lifestyle of material acquisition, engendering, in turn, a loss of moral purpose and commitment.

In such a world a writer will construct a reflection stylistically based on accumulation, but which thematically conveys a moral vacuum: "Une femme inconstante est celle qui n'aime plus; une légère, celle qui déjà en aime un autre; une volage, celle qui ne sait si elle aime et ce qu'elle aime; une indifférente, celle qui n'aime rien" ("Femmes," 24). The degree of verbal accumulation is in inverse proportion to the aphorism's theme of emptiness. Characterization, moreover, relies upon a network of division and distinction. During the classical period, as Michel Foucault has shown, distinction was the principal method for classifying in the natural sciences—"L'identité et ce qui la marque se définissent par le résidu des différences. Un animal ou une plante n'est pas ce qu' indique—ou trahit—le stigmate qu'on découvre imprimé en lui; il est ce que ne sont pas les autres; il n'existe en lui-même qu'à la limite de ce qui s'en distingue."[8] La Bruyère, in "Femmes," 24, utilizes this principle. But the fine distinctions he makes are only among degrees of spiritual and moral emptiness. The author of the *Caractères* is dividing and distinguishing in a void.

La Bruyère's firm insistence on the hollow nature of society characterizes his work and separates him from the writers of the 1660s and 1670s. Those moralists had clearly posed the opposition between self and society, and, in favor of the latter, had sought to control the unreasoning, spontaneous side of man. In the *Caractères* there is an emotional and spiritual vacuum because the moralist no longer perceives the need to battle for some overriding value, more essential than any individual's claims. Jules Brody has suggested that La Bruyère intuitively discerned the final days not only of the noble class but also of *la noblesse*—"la noblesse comme témoignage d'une valeur sociale et morale non-négociable, d'une valeur à proprement parler métaphysique."[9] For the chevalier de Méré, perhaps the most ardent defender of the faith, *l'honnêteté*—the moral system devoted to the preservation of those values—was prized above all else. In La Bruyère's universe there is no struggle to preserve an ideal, and the steady degradation of *l'honnête homme* is one outstanding mark of this metaphysical shift. In a series of short reflections, La Bruyère places *l'honnête homme* ever closer to the pejorative *habile homme*, while increasingly distinguishing him from the exemplary *homme de bien*:

> L'honnête homme tient le milieu entre l'habile homme et l'homme de bien, quoique dans une distance inégale de ces deux extrêmes.
> La distance qu'il y a de l'honnête homme à l'habile homme s'affaiblit de jour à autre, et est sur le point de disparaître.
> L'habile homme est celui qui cache ses passions, qui entend ses intérêts, qui y sacrifie beaucoup de choses, qui a su acquérir du bien ou en conserver.
> L'honnête homme est celui qui ne vole pas sur les grands chemins, et qui ne tue personne, dont les vices enfin ne sont pas scandaleux.
> On connaît assez qu'un homme de bien est honnête homme; mais il est plaisant d'imaginer que tout honnête homme n'est pas homme de bien.
> L'homme de bien est celui qui n'est ni un saint ni un dévot, et qui s'est borné à n'avoir que de la vertu. ("Jugements," 55)

In this social universe, *l'honnête homme*, by virtue of his close association with *l'habile homme*, has become an acquirer, an accumulator. Méré's gentlemanly ideal has been tarnished in a world rapidly moving toward domination by the bourgeoisie.

This class shift shatters other ideals of the classical generation as well. The goal of *ataraxie* has been replaced by the reality of anomie. The "monster" is no longer the untamed force of love, but rather the valueless, machine-like "characters," guided only by their spiritually barren and trivial vision of social success. There may be, as Jules Brody believes, redemption in La Bruyère's praise of unpredictability (at least in matters other than love, where the moralist's tone is far less tolerant). In the *Caractères* tendencies toward automatic behavior are challenged by man's desire for change. Nevertheless, there is a large gap between believing that human worth is in unpredictability and asserting that it lies in the individual living at the peak of his physical and psychic energies. In La Bruyère's book the potential for such vitality is completely undermined by a *morale* of petty social aggrandizement.

Thus although La Bruyère was writing only a decade or two later than the other moralists grouped in this study, he clearly deviated from the classical age's emphasis on control and language, on control through the language of reason and the destruction of courtly love myths. The change is radical, signaling a reformed vision of the individual and his society. And yet, despite the diverging moods, the shifting emphasis, there is one strong, common bond between La Bruyère and his immediate predecessors. All ultimately emphasize the social at the expense of the individual.

La Bruyère, perceiving the potentially negative results of a conforming, overmechanized, and status-oriented society, differs from earlier seventeenth-century French moralists, who sought to create an emotional state unthreatening to individual and social order. The society that La Bruyère depicts is far more trivial than the glamorous, overbearing one portrayed by Mme de Lafayette in the early pages of *La Princesse de Clèves*. But though he may nostalgically regret the loss of individual commitment in a world given over to banal social concerns, La Bruyère, at the same time, is intellectually captivated by society's hold.

The general direction of social gravitation in the *Caractères* is toward the monarch, or at least toward the arena where he presides, the court. In both the provinces and the city, *la cour* represents the epitome of social success; and for those already there (the courtiers), proximity to the monarch is the sign of one's standing. It has long been a commonplace in La Bruyère scholarship that the chapter on the sovereign figures at the center of the *Caractères*, thereby transmitting a strong sense of order and authority that inherently limit the individual's importance. There is, moreover, no real challenge to the monarch's authority in La Bruyère's book. Despite the admittedly trivial nature of life at the court, the sovereign's command is unquestioned. That the courtier is frequently ludicrous in his efforts to be "placed" does not detract from an awareness of the monarch's total control.

With the generation of moralists who preceded La Bruyère, social order and authority may sometimes be less obviously prominent. Although strongly evident in writers such as Mme de Lafayette and Guilleragues, allusions to absolute rule may be perceived less directly in Jacques Esprit's work or in the writings of the chevalier de Méré. Nevertheless, even when forthright allusions to the monarchy are shunned, it is impossible to ignore the moral authoritarianism of these works. The repression of individual and highly intense emotion, the yearning for repose, that dominate the classical generation's moralist literature parallel the growth of French absolutism. In La Bruyère's work the need for repression diminishes, since the individual is no longer a threat to the social universe portrayed by the moralist. Instead, the *Caractères* paint a picture of man identifying totally with society's norms and demands. But this complete adjustment of goals only serves to strengthen the mood of authoritarianism. The diminished stress on individual claims to life in the age's writings, from Saint-Evremond and Méré up through La Bruyère, suggests an effort toward containing emotional freedom, an effort that, moreover, stands in direct opposition to the reality of sexual mores in the *grand siècle*. It was not, however, reality that the moralists sought to depict. Rather, their works offer the vision, conscious or unconscious, of that reality controlled in favor of what the age perceived to be as higher ideals.

1. Peter Brooks, *The Novel of Worldliness* (Princeton, N.J.: Princeton University Press, 1969), p. 77.

2. "Sur le style de La Bruyère," *L'Esprit créateur* 11 (Summer 1971): 167.

3. Ibid., p. 168. All references are to the *Caractères*, ed. Robert Garapon (Paris: Garnier, 1962); subsequent references, consisting of chapter and entry number, will be found in the text.

4. Quoted in Brody, "Images de l'homme chez La Bruyère," *L'Esprit créateur* 15 (Spring-Summer, 1975): 164.

5. René Jasinski, *Deux accès à La Bruyère* (Paris: Minard, 1971), part 2, chaps. 3 and 4.

6. La Rochefoucauld, *Maximes*, ed. Jacques Truchet (Paris: Garnier, 1967), p. 110. Subsequent references are to the maxim number, and will be found in the text. Pascal, *Discours sur les passions de l'amour* (Paris: Hachette, 1966), p. 124.

7. Jasinski, *Deux accès à La Bruyère*, p. 237.

8. Michel Foucault, *Les Mots et les choses* (Paris: Gallimard, 1966), p. 157.

9. Brody, "Sur le style de La Bruyère," p. 167.

# BIBLIOGRAPHY

*Texts*

Descartes, René. *Les Passions de l'âme*. Preface by Samuel Sylvestre de Sacy. Paris: Gallimard, 1953; preface, 1969.

Esprit, Jacques. *La Fausseté des vertus humaines*. 2 vols. Paris, 1678.

Méré, Antoine Gombaud, chevalier de. *Oeuvres complètes*. Edited by Charles-H. Boudhors. 3 vols. Paris: Editions Fernand Roches, 1930.

———. *Lettres*. Paris, 1689.

———. *Maximes, sentences et réflexions morales et politiques*. Paris, 1687.

Guilleragues, Gabriel Joseph de Lavergne, comte de. *Lettres portugaises*. Edited by F. Deloffre and J. Rougeot. Paris: Garnier Frères, 1962.

———. *Valentins*. Edited by F. Deloffre and J. Rougeot. Paris: Garnier Frères, 1962.

La Bruyère, Jean de. *Caractères*. Edited by R. Garapon. Paris: Garnier Frères, 1962.

Lafayette, Marie-Madeleine Pioche de La Vergne, comtesse de. *Histoire de Madame Henriette d'Angleterre, suivie de Mémoires de la cour de France pour les années 1688 et 1689*. Edited by Gilbert Sigaux. Paris: Mercure de France, 1965.

———. *Romans et nouvelles*. Edited by Emile Magne. Paris: Garnier Frères, 1970.

La Rochefoucauld, François VI, duc de. *La Justification de l'amour.* Edited by J. D. Hubert. Paris: A.-G. Nizet, 1971.

————. *Maximes.* Edited by Jacques Truchet. Paris: Garnier Frères, 1967.

Pascal, Blaise. *Pensées et opuscules.* Edited by Léon Brunschvicg. Paris: Classiques Hachette, 1966; original edition, 1897.

Saint-Evremond, Charles de Marguetel de Saint-Denis, seigneur de. *Lettres.* Edited by René Ternois. 2 vols. Paris: Librairie Marcel Didier, 1967-68.

————. *Oeuvres.* 7 vols. London: Tonson, 1711.

Sévigné, Marie de Rabutin-Chantal, marquise de. *Lettres.* Edited by Gérard-Gailly. 3 vols. Paris: Bibliothèque de la Pléiade, 1953.

*Works Referred to or Consulted*

Adam, Antoine. *Histoire de la littérature française au XVII^e siècle.* 5 vols. Paris: Domat, 1948-62.

Allentuch, Harriet Ray. *Madame de Sévigné: A Portrait in Letters.* Baltimore: Johns Hopkins University Press, 1963.

Aveline, Claude. *Et tout le reste n'est rien.* Paris: Mercure de France, 1951.

Barnwell, H. T. *Les Idées morales et critiques de Saint-Evremond.* Paris: Presses universitaires de France, 1957.

Barthes, Roland. *Essais critiques.* Paris: Editions du Seuil, 1964.

Baumal, Francis. *Le Féminisme au temps de Molière.* Paris: Renaissance du livre, 1926.

Bénichou, Paul. *Morales du grand siècle.* Paris: Gallimard, 1948.

Borgerhoff, E. B. O. *The Freedom of French Classicism.* Princeton, N.J.: Princeton University Press, 1950.

Bounoure, Gabriel. "La Perle blanche." *Mercure de France,* No. 1213 (November 1964), pp. 426-35.

Bray, Bernard. *L'Art de la lettre amoureuse.* The Hague: Mouton, 1967.

————. "Quelques aspects du système épistolaire de Mme de Sévigné." *Revue d'histoire littéraire de la France* 69 (May-August 1969): 491-505.

Brémond, Henri. *Histoire littéraire du sentiment religieux en France.* Vol. 1. *L'Humanisme dévot.* Paris: Bloud & Gay, 1916.

Brody, Jules. "*La Princesse de Clèves* and the Myth of Courtly Love." *University of Toronto Quarterly* 38 (January 1969): 105-35.

————. "Sur le style de La Bruyère." *L'Esprit créateur* 11 (Summer 1971): 154-68.

————. "Images de l'homme chez La Bruyère." *L'Esprit créateur* 15 (Spring-Summer 1975): 164-88.

Brooks, Peter. *The Novel of Worldliness*. Princeton, N.J.: Princeton University Press, 1969.

Brown, Norman O. *Life against Death*. Middletown, Conn.: Wesleyan University Press, 1959.

Brunschvicg, Léon. *Spinoza et ses contemporains*. 3d ed. Paris: F. Alcan, 1923.

Busson, Henri. *La Religion des classiques*. Paris: Presses universitaires de France, 1948.

Butor, Michel. *Répertoire*. Paris: Editions de Minuit, 1960.

Butrick, May Wendelene. "The Concept of Love in the *Maxims* of La Rochefoucauld." Ph.D. diss., State University of Iowa, 1959.

Carré, Marie-Rose. "La Rencontre inachevée: étude sur la structure de *La Princesse de Clèves*. PMLA 87 (May 1972): 475-82.

Chamaillard, Edmond. *Le Chevalier de Méré, suivi d'un choix de lettres et de pensées du chevalier*. Paris: G. Clouzot, 1921.

Chuppeau, J. "Remarques sur la genèse des 'Lettres portugaises.' " *Revue d'histoire littéraire de la France* 69 (May-August 1969): 506-24.

Cohen, Gustave. *Le Séjour de Saint-Evremond en Hollande et l'entrée de Spinoza dans le champ de la pensée française*. Paris: Champion, 1926.

Cordelier, Jean. *Mme de Sévigné par elle-même*. Paris: Editions du Seuil, 1967.

Doubrovsky, Serge. "*La Princesse de Clèves*: une interprétation existentielle." *Table ronde*, No. 138 (June 1959), pp. 36-51.

Du Bled, Victor. *La Société française du XVI$^e$ siècle au XX$^e$ siècle*. 4th ser. (seventeenth century). Paris: Perrin et Cie, 1904.

Duchêne, Roger. *Réalité vécue et art épistolaire: Madame de Sévigné et la lettre d'amour*. Paris: Bordas, 1970.

Dulong, Claude. *L'Amour au XVII$^e$ siècle*. Paris: Hachette, 1969.

Durry, Marie Jeanne. *Madame de Lafayette.* Paris: Mercure de France, 1962.

Fagniez, Gustave. *La Femme et la société française dans la première motié du XVIIᵉ siècle.* Paris: J. Gamber, 1929.

Foucault, Michel. *Les Mots et les choses.* Paris: Gallimard, 1966.

Freud, Sigmund. *Civilization and Its Discontents.* Edited by James Strachey. New York: W. W. Norton & Co., 1961.

Green, F. C. "Who Was the Author of the 'Lettres Portugaises'?" *Modern Language Review* 21 (1926): 159-67.

Harth, Erica. "Exorcising the Beast: Attempts at Rationality in French Classicism." *PMLA* 88 (January 1973): 19-24.

Hippeau, Louis. *Essai sur la morale de La Rochefoucauld.* Paris: A. G. Nizet, 1967.

Hoog, Armand. "Sacrifice d'une Princesse." *La Nef* 6 (July 1949): 16-25.

Jasinski, René. *Deux accès à La Bruyère.* Paris: Minard, 1971.

Knapp, Bettina L. *Jean Racine: Mythos and Renewal in Modern Theatre.* University, Ala.: University of Alabama Press, 1971.

Krailsheimer, A. J. *Studies in Self-Interest: From Descartes to La Bruyère.* Oxford: Clarendon Press, 1962.

Lafuma, Louis. "Introduction." Blaise Pascal, *Discours sur les passions de l'amour.* Edited by Louis Lafuma. Paris: Delmas, 1950.

Lanson, Gustave. *Choix de lettres du dix-septième siècle.* Paris: Hachette, 1913.

Lewis, Philip. "La Rochefoucauld: The Rationality of Play." *Yale French Studies*, No. 41 (1964), pp. 133-47.

Magendie, Maurice. *La Politesse mondaine et les théories de l'honnêteté en France au XVIIᵉ siècle, de 1600 á 1660.* 2 vols. in 1. Geneva: Slatkine Reprints, 1970.

Marcu, Eva. "Madame de Sévigné and Her Daughter." *Romanic Review* 51 (October 1960): 182-91.

Mauron, Charles. *L'Inconscient dans l'oeuvre et la vie de Racine.* Aix-en-Provence: Publication des Annales de la Faculté des Lettres, 1957.

Miloyevitch, Youkossava. *La Théorie des passions du P. Senault* *et la morale chrétienne en France au XVII<sup>e</sup> siècle.* Paris: L. Rodstein, 1935.

Mongrédien, Georges. *Le XVII<sup>e</sup> Siècle galant: libertins et amoureuses.* Paris: Perrin et Cie, 1929.

Moore, Will G. *French Classical Literature.* London: Oxford University Press, 1961.

————. "La Rochefoucauld: une nouvelle anthropologie." *Revue des sciences humaines,* No. 72 (October-December 1953), pp. 301-10.

Mornet, Daniel. *Histoire de la littérature française classique, 1660-1700.* Paris: Armand Colin, 1942.

Nadal, Octave. *Le Sentiment de l'amour dans l'oeuvre de Pierre Corneille.* Paris: Gallimard, 1948.

Payer, Alice de. *Le Féminisme au temps de la Fronde.* Paris: Société des éditions Fast, 1922.

Peyre, Henri. *Qu'est-ce que le classicisme?* Paris: A. G. Nizet, 1964.

Pingaud, Bernard. *Mme de Lafayette par elle-même.* Paris: Editions du Seuil, 1959.

Pintard, René. *Le Libertinage érudit dans la première moitié du XVII<sup>e</sup> siècle.* 2 vols. Paris: Boivin, 1943.

Poulet, Georges. *Etudes sur le temps humain.* Paris: Plon, 1950.

Racine, Jean. *Théâtre complet.* Edited by Maurice Rat. Paris: Garnier Frères, 1960.

Rosmarin, Leonard. "The Unsublimated Libido: Saint-Evremond's Conception of Love." *French Review* 46 (December 1972): 263-70.

Rougemont, Denis de. *L'Amour et l'occident.* Paris: 10/18, 1962 (original edition: Plon, 1939).

Rousset, Jean. *Forme et signification.* Paris: José Corti, 1962.

Schmidt, Albert Marie. *Saint-Evremond ou l'humaniste impur.* Paris: Editions du Cavalier, 1932.

Spitzer, Leo. "Les 'Lettres Portugaises.' " *Romanische Forschungen* 65 (1953): 94-135.

Starobinski, Jean. "Complexité de La Rochefoucauld." *Preuves,* No. 135 (May 1962), pp. 33-40.

————. "La Rochefoucauld et les morales substitutives." *Nouvelle revue française* 14 (July 1966): 16-34; (August 1966): 211-29.

Strowski, Fortunat J. *La Sagesse française (Montaigne, Saint-François de Sales, Descartes, La Rochefoucauld, Pascal).* Paris: Plon-Nourrit, 1925.

Viguié, Pierre. *L'Honnête Homme au XVII$^e$ siècle: le chevalier de Méré (1607-1684).* Paris: R. Chiberre, 1922.

# INDEX

Not included in this index are essential key words which appear virtually everywhere in the text: love, passion, language, control, Eros, pleasure, self.